An Unfinished Marriage

Also by Joan Anderson
in Large Print:

A Year by the Sea

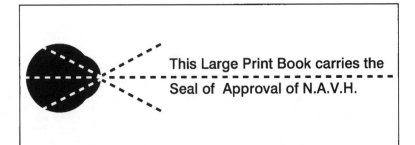

This Large Print Book carries the
Seal of Approval of N.A.V.H.

An
Unfinished
Marriage

Joan Anderson

WHEELER
PUBLISHING

This memoir is a memory of a particular time in my life during which certain experiences and persons contributed to my perspective and thus altered the manner in which I approach life today.
In some cases, names and identifying characteristics have been changed to protect the privacy of those involved. In addition, I have telescoped several events or people to more fully concentrate a point.

Published in 2002 by arrangement with Doubleday, a division of the Doubleday Broadway Publishing Group, a division of Random House Inc.

Wheeler Hardcover Series.

The text of this Large Print edition is unabridged.
Other aspects of the book may vary from the original edition.

Photograph by John P. Kelly/Image Bank.

Set in 16 pt. Plantin by Rick Gundberg.

Printed in the United States on permanent paper.

**Library of Congress Control Number: 2002105936
ISBN: 1-58724-259-1 (lg. print : hc : alk. paper)**

For my unfinished man
JA

Every beginning is always a sequel,
after all, and the book of events is
always open halfway through.

— Wislawa Szymborska,
"Love at First Sight,"
from *View with a Grain of Sand*

Contents

Prologue 9

Chapter One   *Getting Under Way*
                         Late September 15

Chapter Two   *Becoming a Mate, Again*
                         October 29

Chapter Three   *In the Doldrums*
                         Late October 43

Chapter Four   *Setting the Course*
                         Mid-November 63

Chapter Five   *The Wind at My Back*
                         Early December 87

Chapter Six   *Buoyed*
                         Christmas Eve 109

Chapter Seven   *Riding the Storm*
                         Late January 131

Chapter Eight   *Dropping Anchor*
                         Late March 151

Chapter Nine   *All Hands on Deck*
                         May 167

Chapter Ten   *Shacking Up*
                         June 183

Chapter Eleven *Safe Harbor*
            Later in June 199
Chapter Twelve *Forever at Sea*
            Late July 219

Acknowledgments 232

Prologue

Never did I think when I ran away from home that a memoir, *A Year by the Sea*, would come from that experience, nor did I expect that thousands of women would write to tell me that my experience was their experience.

I had taken a "vacation from marriage," a sabbatical of sorts, during which I hoped to reclaim that raw-material person I had left behind in my youth before I started to play the roles our culture demands of women. It was a bold gesture choosing not to follow my husband to his new job and suggesting instead that I spend some time at our spartan Cape Cod cottage. Some women friends called me brave, others thought I was crazy, and the husbands of most disapproved heartily.

But for once, I didn't take into account what others thought. Determined to shake up my dull life, I was working on pure gut reaction. Words have a peculiar way of slipping out of my mouth before they are formed, and so, when I announced my intention to my husband, I shocked us both. It wasn't until I was standing on the shoreline of my favorite beach that I began to realize the ramifications of my impulsive decision. I had altered my life and was left holding freedom in one hand and guilt in the other.

As resident nurturer of a family of four, I had spent the past thirty years sustaining others while neglecting myself in the process. Now, it was my turn to retreat, repair, and, I hoped, regenerate myself. Was I being selfish or smart? Fortunately, the feminist writer Adrienne Rich answered my question in her book *Of Woman Born*, where she points out that primitive tribes send their women away "to go down into herself, to introvert, in order to evoke her instincts and intuitions," strengths that these cultures value in women.

Perhaps an inner voice was leading me, I thought. Perhaps living apart from people and daily agendas would allow me to reconnect to the internal strengths that once were mine. In any case, alone and temporarily independent, I would have no choice but to be both conscious and aware of what my new world would present. I was ebbing like the tide as it turns itself around — not coming in or going out — and, as such, I was being made to follow the rules of the universe rather than those of the society.

In a world of broad strokes and neon signs, we tend to forget that true learning comes from our own impulses. The secular age provides few tools to help us interpret the experience of life.

Change begins with taking ourselves away from the clutter in order to hear what one's heart needs to say. Many messages and messengers came to me once I was able to relinquish control and offer myself up to serendipity. A chance encounter with a colony of seals alerted me to what was missing in my life — things like playfulness, vulnerability, mystery, adventure, being at home in my body, and undomestication. Befriending ninety-two-year-old Joan Erikson, wife of the psychoanalyst Erik Erikson, offered me untold wisdom about the meaning of identity and life's stages. Being forced to earn a living and getting a job in a fish market taught me the worth of using my body instead of just my mind. And then there were the long walks into the elements, where the seasons and the shore offered metaphors that helped me understand that all would be mine in its time and season and that relationships and experiences would become fluid only if I were patient enough to wait for the thaw.

In reflecting back on my year by the sea, I realize how much it was about saying yes to such things as spontaneity, risk taking, instincts, and, of course, the natural world. I continue to revel in raw experiences that heighten the intensity of my days — not unlike a child who is guided by her wonder and curiosity. What has developed over time is a kind of knowing that doesn't involve my head but rather my senses. I've come to understand that I am as unfinished as the shoreline along the beach. What's more, my husband, my two sons, and their wives are equally unfinished. That is the great message . . . to transcend ourselves again and again and to know that those with whom we come in contact are in process as well.

Having reinstated a relationship with myself, it was time for the greater challenge — that of reconnecting with another. The reassembling of my marriage would have never happened without my year of solitude. Taking time away from each other was, in retrospect, both necessary and appropriate.

After the initial shock, anger, and discord that occurred around the separation abated, my husband took a penetrating look at those experiences most would choose to bury — weeding out self-indulgence and wishful thinking — in order to determine his destiny with or without me. What role, if any, did he play in this turn of events, he asked himself. How much of my decision had to do with his lassitude? Once apart, was his preference to be alone or together?

There was no question that we both needed the space to understand the roots of our relationship and the values around what we had created together. We had become estranged for reasons no more complicated than laziness, indifference, and ignorance. In deciding to recommit, we also desired to fight for an openness in which the faults of the other could be admitted; by doing so, we could unlearn that which keeps us away from the immediacy of our lives and our connection with each other.

So began the continuation of our marriage, minus the fire of old passion and mired with problems and illusions. In *The Art of Loving*, Erich Fromm says, "Nothing, especially love, can be mastered without practice — and practice involves discipline, concentration, patience, and supreme concern." Through trial and error, yielding and resisting, retracing and reinventing, dependence and interdependence, we began the task of reassembling our lives together. The year was spent crawling toward the inexpressible. There was no model to follow. We were two unique souls who merged over thirty years ago, and *out of* that union appeared an original couple, impossible to replicate. *Out of* our vulnerabilities a new way of being together needed to be discovered. The unfinished elements of our relationship will forever rise and fall, like the incoming tide, constantly and irresistibly moving within us.

1

Getting Under Way

LATE SEPTEMBER

The beginnings . . . of all human
undertakings are untidy.

— John Galsworthy

The night sky has barely dissolved to a pale blue light when I slide out of bed and tiptoe to the kitchen, relishing the early-morning silence I have come to treasure. This is when my thinking is clearest, when I give over to the spirits in the air and let them direct my day. My husband, Robin, seems to know that I need this time and frequently rolls over in continued sleep until I am out the door for my morning walk.

I put the kettle on the stove and wait for its wail while the threadbare afghan I grabbed from the couch warms my shoulders. A few minutes later, steaming coffee in hand, I ease open the screen door, stifling its inevitable creak, step into the morning dew, and take a deep breath of Cape Cod air. Several birds are nibbling at their feeder while the neighbor's cat huddles under a bayberry bush waiting to pounce. As I sink onto the stoop, I let the sensuousness of my surroundings take over. The clarity of morning always offers a fresh start.

We've been back together some three weeks

now after a yearlong separation. The decision to reconcile happened as precipitously as the decision to separate. He was able to take early retirement and, having watched me grow and change from afar, seemed anxious to get on with the adventure of his own unlived life. Having acquired a much stronger sense of self during my solitary year by the sea, I seemed to have an inexplicable compulsion to return to living with another. Once the decision to reunite was made, we slid back into relationship with little fanfare and even less preparation. Call us stubborn, karmically connected, or just plain stupid, it appears that we plan to slug it out *till death do us part.* But I wonder if it is not so much about the power of our love as it is about the strength of old friendship.

Even so, I enjoyed the vagaries of single life and am unnerved at being coupled again. This lack of ease makes me feel like the innocent I was when I flew off some thirty years ago to marry this man in faraway East Africa. We had met at Yale Drama School and soon thereafter realized how impossible it would be to try to survive in the theater with no guaranteed income, to say nothing of steady employment. Joining the Peace Corps seemed to offer a solution. It wasn't difficult to choose adventure over starvation, especially since there were so many illusions and hopes attached to my blushing virginity. I had an entire life spread out before me with plenty of time for trial and error. Now such innocence is gone, and I'm more practical, less expectant, and painfully aware that I'm supposed to know not only what marriage is all about but also how to live gracefully within its walls. Everything has become strangely reconfigured, and in the process I've been rendered anxious.

I recall asking my uncle for marital advice before heading down the aisle. He handed me a passage from *The Prophet* in which Kahlil Gibran likens matrimony to the oak and the cypress trees: "Stand together, yet not too near — for the pillars of the temple stand apart and the oak and the cypress grow not in each other's shadow." Perhaps unknowingly, I took the prophet's advice when I *ran away* from home last year. The institution of marriage had permeated my very being; my focus was always on "us," so that I became incapable of being conscious of "me." Devoted as I was to the role of good wife and helpmate, I worked mostly in my husband's shadow, until a sort of toxicity set in that poisoned the air we breathed. By the time I left, we had become more like incestuous siblings than husband and wife.

I suppose that is why we now seem to be giving each other room, fighting against a life of routine, facing each other with both detachment and cautious acceptance. By the time I return from my walk, Robin is generally off to the golf course, which is revitalizing his sedentary body. I'm uncomfortable that our instincts seem to take us in such divergent directions, and yet I

sense that we both know that too much togetherness might strip away the new individuality
we've each recently cultivated. Finding personal
space within perpetual togetherness is key. It
might appear that we are trying to avoid one another, but in fact we are both intent on creating
new lives. I am determined for us not to become
one of those vacant couples you see in restau-
rants, heads buried in their meals, looking as if
all vitality and essence had been sucked out of
them. Not me! Not that! I think he shares my
sense that we need to create new independent
lives, so that when we return home in the evening we each bring a vibrancy that comes from
meaningful endeavor.

Still, I wonder how to get the marriage back on
track. Where are the guidebooks for maintaining
relationships? There is a plethora of prescrip-
tions for raising children, getting jobs, being sexual, and understanding the self. But veterans of
long-term marriage, deserted by their youthful
hormones, are left to muddle along in their mid-
dle-aged bodies. In due time I expect some modicum of happiness to surface. At least I hope so,
because at our age we don't have days to squan-
der.

As the sun climbs above the trees, I am eager
to turn from such troubling thoughts and more
than ready to embrace the wild land beyond my
door. I go inside to retrieve my jeans and
sweater, lace up my sneakers, and head out toward the dirt path I have walked hundreds of

times, reminding myself of the Navajo saying: The sun has only one day. Live this day in a good way so that the sun won't have wasted precious time.

The forest is alive with the sound of rustling creatures scurrying under fallen leaves and acorns being squashed underfoot. These external noises drown out my internal chatter. But not five minutes down the lane, my tranquillity is jarred by the sound of a huge engine, and I quickly spot the source: a North American Van Lines truck, inching its way up our narrow path, breaking branches as it heads straight toward me. Interrupting the normally quiet woods, the truck appears like an unwelcome mirage. Nonetheless, I step into the brush and out of the way as I hear Robin's voice and see him running through the woods, buckling his trousers while shoving his feet into his Dock-Siders.

"Is this truck for us?" I ask incredulously.

"Yep," he assures me. "Just stuff from the office."

"The office!" I counter, my tone edgy and tense. "Didn't you leave all that behind?"

"Not my files and furniture," he answers, a curt tone now creeping into the conversation. I back away from a potential confrontation, reminding myself of my silent promise not to instruct him or ask too many questions. Men dislike instruction, my mother told me. They've had enough of it from their mothers and teachers. If I can hold my tongue, he might figure out,

21

independent of me, how to get on with his life. Besides, I've come to know that I can have power or love — but not both. This time I'm after love.

Three young men hop out of the cab and open the side door of the van, as Robin tells them to put the cartons inside the living room. "Just stack them up along the one empty wall," he says, to my irritation, without a glance in my direction.

My heart sinks. In the past year I have tried to create a Zen-like space in our little cottage, and soon, it appears, that will be undone. When he filled the guest-room closet with ties, suits, shoes, and golfing paraphernalia, I figured it was only a matter of time before he would drop the buttoned-up look and settle into casual clothes. But when he declared the basement his exclusive domain and ordered a new desk and file cabinet soon thereafter, I was more than alarmed. His spending spree reminded me more of a bored housewife than a man suddenly free of daily drudgery.

I watch as box after box is carried from the truck and will myself to believe that he has a plan for his new life. With that thought, I stride off through a tunnel of trees certain that motion will quell my internal disturbance. But halfway up the road, I'm besieged again with unkind thoughts and wonder about the source of my anger. If I loved this cottage best when it bustled with family and friends, why would I now bristle at the intrusion of one? Certainly living apart has made both of us more territorial, but there's plenty of room left for coexistence. I'm feeling invaded, but how could that be? He is, after all, my husband! Besides, haven't I learned after all these years that men come rushing into homes with gusto? Unaccustomed as they are to sleeping babies, meditative states, and everyone else's space, they stomp about, slam doors, and crank up the stereo. Such behavior comes with the territory.

Mercifully my walk takes me out of the woods and into a meadow where the edges of things begin to soften, as does my heart. I hadn't wanted to assume what our life would be like when Robin joined me, and I'm not about to start now. Poor fellow. Giving up a secure job for an unknown future is bound to have some ramifications. For the past thirty years, the better part of his days has been spent within four walls of a small office. Having broken free, he must wonder if he's in exile or under house arrest. One of my tasks as a "recovering wife" is to be gracious and accommodating, even if it feels like adjusting to the strange habits of a college roommate. After all, it took me a year to rid myself of the old and permit new attitudes to surface. He needs the same amount of latitude to stumble into his old self again.

I take a deep breath and forge on, up a gradual incline toward the shoulder of a hill where the view forces me to stop, breathe, and be grateful.

This must be the most gentle and beautiful morning so far this fall — golden and mellow, as the chilly air quickly becomes warm. My irritable mood drifts away like the falling leaves. Today the trees display deepening hues — mauve, beige, sage, and gray — subtle tones that calm my spirit and remind me of where I am in my life.

I spot a huge pile of leaves and topple into its center, overcome by this season's message. Fall is about coming full circle. It indicates the culmination of birth, growth, and death — not unlike couples who have endured myriad challenges only to arrive at the autumn of their lives. I finger the leaves surrounding me, their patterns and colors individual, varied, and vibrant, and remember, as a child, how I had wanted to preserve their glory by ironing each carefully chosen leaf between pieces of waxed paper.

It occurs to me that if I want to know the moments as well as digest my experiences, I have to give it time. Our marriage as it was is over. But our relationship as it is, ripened and weathered, has a deeper tone to it — not unlike these wonderfully rich colored leaves that half the world pays homage to each September and October. Moreover, since Robin and I have chosen to reassemble our relationship in a bucolic setting, on our own steam, minus the rules and constraints of a staid society, we are left to receive that which will evolve from our own natural cycles.

I like where my thoughts are taking me. This

place and my walk have once again worked their magic. I have regained my balance. Returning to the cottage will be full of affirming thoughts. My stomach growls as I turn back toward home, quickening my step as the road tilts upward until I arrive at the kitchen door.

With no sign of the truck or my husband, I duck into the outside shower to rinse off not only the grit collected on the walk but the remnants of an impulse to control left over from my solitary life. As the clear, hot water releases the tension from my shoulders, I gaze up at the blue sky and let my immediate and selfish desires wash down the drain. Feeling cleansed, I step from the stall just as I hear the ringing of the phone and duck inside the back door to answer it. It's my friend Charlotte. "How's it going?" she whispers, as if asking for secret information.

I sigh, exasperated all over again, and tell her that right now I'm feeling crowded. "Robin's moved his entire office into the cottage," I say.

"His what? I thought he retired."

"Ah, so did I," I continue, "but I suppose he's hoping to consult or run educational seminars and wants to make sure his books and papers are available."

"Isn't he supposed to be creating a new life?" she asks, remembering some of Robin's and my conversations as we daydreamed about world travel, living abroad a few months of the year, or working for an organization such as the National Audubon Society.

"I'm giving him a long leash," I say. "Whatever he said before he arrived has changed with the reality of being here. On my walk today I found myself feeling his pain — recalling the early days of withdrawal from my old life. I remember how lonely change can be."

"You sound like you're getting soft," she goads. "Do I smell the rekindling of some sort of romance?"

"Hardly," I chuckle. "It's about relearning what it is to be married without the budding hormones! A sort of androgyny has set in. We're warming up slowly. One minute it feels familiar and the next kind of strange, like we're on a blind date."

"They were scary," she says with her usual sardonic wit.

"No kidding," I agree. "We've been taking in matinees and then going out for a bowl of chowder — benign activities to be sure, but they keep us relating, nonetheless."

Uncomfortable with how this conversation is going, and freezing now clad only in my damp towel, I beg off, promising to keep her posted on each new installment. I hang up feeling like a guinea pig in this remarriage business. It was hard enough explaining to everyone why I ran away last year and now even more complicated trying to make someone understand reconciliation.

I throw on a robe and head for the kitchen, gingerly pulling open the screen door, half afraid of seeing the mess he surely has created. Robin is sitting on the bench beside the kitchen table staring at the contents of one of the boxes.

"Doesn't look like office stuff to me," I say, gazing at the motley collection of old things — a rusty Slinky, magic card tricks, marbles mixed up with foreign coins, World War II medals, and some arrowheads.

"This is a box of my treasures," he says, "from when I was a kid. I kept them hidden under a loose floorboard in my bedroom. Never showed them to a soul."

"Oh yes you did," I say, remembering our courtship days when we visited his family homestead and he led me to the attic and the very place where his secret things were stored. I am seduced by his vulnerability, but rather than going to him I reach for the Slinky, tossing it from hand to hand while mulling over my feelings. Life has a way of sustaining the vulnerable child in each of us, preserving our tender parts, healing the wounds inflicted by separation and transition.

As quiet descends, he seems embarrassed and quickly begins packing his trinkets back into the cigar box. For a split second I feel a sense of intimacy that I haven't felt for a while. A few embers of kinship seem to be warming up our connection. I'm counting on such tenderness to reappear from time to time.

2

Becoming a Mate, Again

OCTOBER

Men and women should never try to conform to one another — they should complement each other.

— Florida Scott Maxwell,
Women, and Sometimes Men

It is a rainy morning. I awake to the aroma from a steaming cup of coffee Robin has placed on my bedside table. He tucks several pillows behind my head and shoulders and whispers good morning. Propped up and staring at the stormy dawn, I'm reminded of days gone by when he would bring me coffee and dress for work, all the while carrying on a conversation about the things that were happening in both of our lives. I've often thought that this one daily ritual strengthened the marriage more than any other, and that as the boys listened from their nearby rooms, the familiar sounds of our muffled conversations must have given them a sense of security.

Today's ramblings begin with thoughts of renovating the cottage. Gradually our discussion moves to the larger issue of money, or the lack thereof. Unbeknownst to me, Robin has been perusing periodicals — *House Beautiful*, *Country Home*, *Architectural Digest* — and coming up with some grand plans. He's envisioning lifting the roof, creating dormers, and adding on a substantial kitchen and family room. He even has pictures, torn from the magazines, that depict the direction his thoughts are taking.

Sad to say, I can't get excited just now. I'm feeling the financial pinch of his retirement and am somewhat surprised that he seems unaffected. A month ago he produced an antique tin box in which he suggested we keep our spending money. "Like we did in the old days," he said, recalling happier but poorer times. I found the gesture charming, but by month's end, I grew tired of staring at an empty box.

"How are we going to finance an addition?" I ask. "Your pension check barely covers the household bills. How would we manage an even bigger place?"

"We have the profit from the sale of our old house just sitting in the bank," he answers, sounding not one bit defensive. "That should cover what I have in mind."

"How can you be so confident?" I counter, edgy yet hating myself for dampening his enthusiasm and being so negative.

"I've talked to a couple of builders . . . been crunching the numbers. It's doable," he says, and then adds, "I'm assuming you'll be going back to your old job at the fish market. Of course I intend to find some sort of job, too."

I recoil at the thought. The fish market! That was necessary employment last year when I was living alone and trying to make ends meet. But continuing such backbreaking work was not the plan I had in mind. "How about cashing in some of your bank stock," I suggest. "After all, your parents gave us the land this cottage sits on as a wedding gift. Wouldn't it be appropriate to put your inheritance toward finishing the job?"

"We're not using the bank stock," Robin asserts swiftly and firmly, a dissonance creeping into the conversation. "That's for our nursing home days."

"Nursing home days! Oh, please," I retort and then sink back into myself. How could such a hopeful morning dissolve to this? Must harmony always be so illusory? Just when I think we're on the same path, communication goes astray. I hate for the day to take such a turn. It's Sunday — perfect for brunch, the *New York Times*, a fire, and warm feelings. Perhaps Robin feels the same way for he quickly leaves the bedroom to get us each another cup of coffee.

I long for a brick wall against which I can bang my head, but I settle for the headboard. Skilled as I am at adapting and improvising, I don't have the stomach for it today. Whatever happened to us, anyway? Who took the magic out of it? I suppose the reason why I saw the movie *Shirley Valentine* five times was because she, too, wondered where her marriage had gone. "Just one day it wasn't the same," she said. "The trouble is, I can't remember when it went wrong." So many pivotal moments occur over the course of a marriage, and there is rarely any forewarning that things are headed into a downward spiral.

In the early years I felt invincible, knowing that I could rehearse, readjust, reconfigure any scene. Now it seems that my belief systems were based on Tinker Bell's fairy dust, magic wands, and during more dire times, the faith that I could call on God for a miracle or two. But age brings with it the stolid reality that there are no sudden transformations, that the real work of becoming a couple never ends, and that even though we've been married for half our lives, we still haven't figured out how to get it right. I remember dressing for my wedding and whispering to my sister-in-law, who was my matron of honor, that I was anxious. "Don't be scared," she answered, as I hung on her every word. She must know, I thought; she's been married an entire year and a half. "No one knows how to be married. You just do it and figure it out as you go along."

I was nervous then, but also full of anticipation. Now the anticipation has been replaced with resignation. I'm ashamed to admit that being a couple once again feels like a hindrance. As a practice of common courtesy, Robin and I inform each other of our plans for the day. It's a small gesture, to be sure, but compared with the freedom of last year, such behavior cramps my style. Then, my instincts and moods offered serendipity to my days. I did as I pleased, followed my whims, reflected on the muse, all of which filled me up much more than this dull marriage does.

One problem is that we aren't having fun yet. Being together day in and day out for the past six weeks has reminded me how very different we really are. Robin likes the house hot, I like it cold; he prefers rock music while I enjoy Baroque; he is a meat-and-potatoes guy, and I'm practically vegetarian. I see objectives to be met while he sees obstacles to be overcome. I'm an optimist, he's a pessimist.

Nowhere are our differences more pronounced than in the bedroom, where they've remained since our wedding night in faraway Africa. We drove several hours to a simple hotel in the bush where twin beds stood waiting, each draped in its own cocoon of mosquito netting. Baffled by the unromantic setting, I retired to the bathroom and left my groom to rearrange the room. I was certain he'd find a way to turn this spartan place into an exotic honeymoon suite. But when I emerged in an off-white peignoir, the beds remained separate, and Robin lay on one of them, motioning for me to join him. I fell into his arms, more able then than I am now to push my disappointments away.

Back in the States, the society page in my hometown newspaper headlined the event: BRIDE TAKEN IN EAST AFRICA. It was strange wording for a wedding announcement, but actually quite to the point. Having never made love before, I felt both unceremoniously deflowered and affirmed. I had spent my youth dreaming about my wedding and the momentous night that would follow. To be taken meant I was chosen, and that was more important than whether or not we agreed on how the scene should be set.

Now other more basic dramas are being played out in the bedroom. Robin wants flannel sheets, I like cotton; he wants the window closed while I need it open; he's a heavy sleeper while I'm a light one and wish I could still turn on the light at three a.m. to read a trashy novel. As for sex, I wonder if I'll ever be taken again! Although there has been some cuddling since his return, we haven't progressed further than that. Curiously our reluctance to make love has less to do with the absence of desire and more to do with my need for comfort. Within a minute or two of an embrace, I often pull away, throw off the blankets, and hug the opposite side of the bed. Between my hot flashes and his body heat, being close just isn't that comfortable. Perhaps these physical changes kick in when passion and fervor are no longer needed to ensure that we procreate the species.

Allowing myself to sit and stew with a series of untidy thoughts is cathartic and usually changes my mood for the better. By the time Robin returns to the bedroom, I want to reassure him that our distress is probably just a sign that something is changing, not that something is wrong.

"I understand, sweetie," he says, using an endearment that lets me know he wants a temporary truce as well. "I probably got carried away thinking about what we could do rather than what is really practical."

"Well, one glance at this magazine, and I'm tempted too," I answer. "Perhaps I should haul out some of my old proposals and see if I can't sell an article or two. I've gotten lazy with my writing."

"Whatever," he says, his voice trailing off in such a way that I know this talk is finished. "I think I'll head out for the paper. Want me to pick up some doughnuts?"

"Fine," I say with some resignation, knowing that the intimate portion of our day has come to a close. The storm is howling now, rain pelting the windows like hail and the screen door flapping in the wind. The weather is as uncontrollable as my thoughts. I wish that, for once, I could stop the questions that fill my mind, but I'm driven to understand this husband of mine and what makes us think we belong back together.

Once downstairs, I toss a couple of logs into the coal stove, throw a sweater over my nightgown, and decide to make another pot of coffee. This morning I can't find the filters because Robin rearranged the kitchen the other day in order to "bond with the house." There are measuring cups where the canned goods used to be, carving knives in the silverware drawer, pots and pans across the room from the stove, and place mats and napkins in the junk drawer — all of this done by a man with the culinary talents of someone who flips burgers at McDonald's. At last I locate the filters under the pot holders and feel as though I've laid my hands on a long-lost puzzle piece. I fill the pot with water, measure out eight spoonfuls of Colombian coffee, and then take refuge in a rocking chair with a pile of airmail letters I sent home from East Africa some thirty years ago. They've been piquing my interest ever since Robin unearthed them from the basement last week. Just now I'm anxious to be reminded of the way we were. This exercise in self-excavation should be amusing.

As I pick through the scenes of a new marriage, I turn up shards of thoughts that make me both laugh and grimace at our naïveté. I'm drawn into the stories, fascinated by my characterization of a youthful husband who sounds glamorous and swashbuckling, a veritable Errol Flynn. "Just plain dashing," I once wrote, "he beguiled everyone with political and historical discourse during a dinner party at the Ambassador's residence." Could that really have been him? The man with whom I've been living avoids gatherings, dreads dinner parties, and is rarely beguiling. I continue reading and am staggered at my pride over his every accomplishment: "He's one of the very best teachers at Kololo, beloved by the students, especially the girls, who frequently send him home with handmade gifts." Even more telling are my descriptions of our day-to-day life: "He helps with setting the table and doing the dishes. He's so giving and we are so happy all the time. Do you realize, Mom and Dad, that we have been married for some five months and still have not had one major fight!" Ridiculous. I was practicing repression from the start.

The next letter describes him as a diligent nursemaid during my bout with malaria: "He brings trays to my bedside without being told. He is taking such good care of me." Not only do I not remember any of these gestures, but the acts that once struck me as so significant now seem pitifully small when compared with what our daughters-in-law expect from our sons.

Rereading the letters, I shake my head at the sham of it all until I begin to sense that my writing these exaggerations was a projection of my wishes. I was describing the characteristics of the man I hoped Robin would become rather than the man he barely was. Every couple in the first bloom of love — that temporary state which tricks people into partnership — believe their feelings to be more reality than illusion, when in fact they're both.

I sit here holding the whole of my conjugal inheritance in a pile of faded airmail letters. We were two souls in search of meaning, attempting to live lives that mattered, united with our dream, unencumbered by the responsibilities of family, not unlike now. As I dig deeper, I discover an even more important truth — living in the wild, so far from friends and family, created an interdependence we would have never achieved if we'd stayed home. This interdependence probably helped us survive the hardships of those beginning years: a fatal automobile accident in which an African man was killed; several burglaries in which thieves took clothes, linens, cameras, anything that they could resell and everything that we couldn't afford to replace; living under a curfew during a tumultuous tribal uprising. Africa saved us from banalities, offering instead living drama that ignited both our spirits and our will.

Back then it didn't seem to matter that we weren't making much money. What mattered was that we were making a difference. At the end of each day we shared tales of my job teaching men to speak English, and his work developing a curriculum designed to make leaders out of Uganda's brightest students.

Suddenly this chilly dark morning is alive with memories. I am fascinated with how we endured those times, now lost but not forgotten. They stand as evidence of our shared idealism and dedication to social causes, and those times most certainly empowered our friendship. As we rebuild our life together, we need to develop some new dreams that might reignite our spirits.

I have a sudden desire to create breakfast. Rummaging through the refrigerator I find eggs, scallions, mushrooms, and cheddar cheese, perfect ingredients for a vegetable omelette. Just as I turn on the radio to the local classical station and

40

start chopping vegetables, I see Robin's car. He scurries up the shell path without the newspaper or the doughnuts. He's been gone for over an hour. What's he been up to, if not errands?

Once he is inside the door, rain dripping off of his yellow slicker, I see he is holding something under his sweater and wearing the mischievous expression of a teenager returning home after an all-nighter. I'm momentarily puzzled, but then I hear a meow.

"I couldn't resist," he says, pulling the ball of coal-black fur out into the open. "There was a lady at the general store with a basket of them," he explains as he strokes the little creature that is shivering with fright. "She said that if you didn't approve, I could bring her back. Isn't she cute?" A warm smile adorns his face — something I haven't seen since he moved here.

"She reminds me of Livingstone," I say, remembering our African cat that was hit by a lorry in front of our hut. "If I touch her, I'll be hooked."

Just then the kitten leaps out of his hands onto the kitchen table and heads straight for me. I reach for the back of her neck, scoop her up, and let her nestle in the crook of my neck. Her purr massages my mind as I sink into the chair. Animals are invaluable conduits. Their antics force us to experience our own dormant emotions. Perhaps Robin knew he needed to refocus. Perhaps the care and feeding of this little animal will nourish both of us.

For now there is a cessation of hostility. Drifting along, without course or direction, is true freedom, an incubator for the care and feeding of new life. I sit with tears of joyful recognition.

3

In the Doldrums

LATE OCTOBER

Learn to lose in order to recover,
and remember that nothing stays the same
for long, not even pain, psychic pain.
Sit it out. Let it all pass. Let it go.

— May Sarton, *Journal of a Solitude*

It's been a tough couple of weeks. Nothing much has progressed between us. Having found an office away from the cottage to insure my perceived independence, I am leaving him space to do as he pleases. Unfortunately we've reverted to behaviors that we fell into before I left — a modicum of pretending, acting like good sports, putting our thoughts and feelings into bright, clean, uncontroversial words. So fearful are we of bad moods or misunderstood statements that we keep ourselves tight and polite, which chafes at me. How I long to slip into an unbearable mood now and again without having to worry that he will take it personally. I am reminded of Anton Chekhov's sentiments: "If you are afraid of loneliness, don't get married."

The truth is I want to drive Robin crazy and scream at the civility of it all in order to feel something other than this status quo. But instead, I take a walk or drive to the pounding surf where I breathe deeply and ask for grace. I suppose I'm still somewhat of a coward, lacking the necessary spontaneous courage that would power my impulses. My actions might symbolize goodness, but the truth is I'm repressing my impatience and frustration. My plan was not to instruct or ask questions. Yet giving him space and respecting his autonomy is only continuing our distance. I yearn to be frank, forthright, and opinionated.

Still, I can't ignore the developments of the last three days. He's taken to bed, working himself into a terminal state of depression. I suspect his frightening lassitude is related to the polite rejections that have been filling our mailbox as a result of the numerous résumés he has sent out. Although these are jobs he has no particular passion to pursue, the mail is demoralizing: "Although your credentials appear impeccable, we have no need for your services at this time." He sits in our bed, unshaven, Coke cans and coffee cups strewn about, his dull eyes peering out from behind tortoiseshell glasses, the classified ads covering the bedspread. The only comfort in this stark scene is the kitten that remains curled up by his feet, intent on staying put until her master decides to resurrect himself. To say that leisure doesn't become him would be an understatement. The plaque, which Charlotte gave me, truly makes sense now: RETIRE-MENT — TWICE AS MUCH HUSBAND FOR HALF AS MUCH MONEY.

It all began a few days ago as we continued the renovation talk. Without warning Robin switched gears. "What am I going to do with all this spare time?" he asked.

I had been expecting this question to surface — dreading it, actually. Obviously I assumed that it was only a matter of time before he found some sort of work, but I kept quiet, wanting him to be the sole designer of his future. Any intervention on my part would surely lead to a rift.

"Give it time," I said, wanting to be prudent in my reply. "Endings must be processed. You can't just leave a career of thirty years and say that's that. This is bound to be one of the biggest transitions you'll ever have to experience."

"That's an understatement," he complained, and I felt a low-grade sense of doom settling in. "Being retired doesn't have much framework. I'm not quite sure who I am anymore."

I bristled at the word *retirement*. To me it has always suggested withdrawal and finality. Having heard of one man who was so bored that he took to arranging stones in a nearby creek, and another who volunteered for so many organizations that his wife barely saw him, I have no patience for retirement talk.

"You aren't really retired," I insisted, pushing the idea away, revealing that I'm more in denial than he is. "You're just changing gears."

"Easy for you to say," Robin countered from between clenched teeth. "When you've been in education all of your life, there aren't tons of people knocking on your door. Anyway, I'd appreciate your patience. I've only been a retired

47

person for a couple of months. How am I supposed to know what to do?"

I was chagrined at the slightest suggestion that I hadn't been patient, not to mention kind and understanding. Yet, this was not the time to insist on defending myself. It was his internal battle, not mine, and besides, talks such as these had backfired in the past. I'd done my time as choreographer of conversations. Not only did I not have the answers to his despair but I felt that he was coming to the misguided conclusion that without a career he faced nothing but a dead end. "Perhaps you should stop thinking about future jobs," I said, "and indulge your whims like I did last year."

Robin said nothing, his body stiffening as he took a swig of coffee. I glanced at his profile and was astonished to realize that after so many years I still haven't an inkling of what is transpiring in his head. As I watched him silently, I began to think it was dumb to mention some of my newly learned lessons because that made me sound as if I held all the answers. Over the years, taking the spotlight off him has been a surefire way to damage his fragile ego. Career and work discussions are always touchy for us. I used to ask a few benign questions in an effort to show an interest in his predicament only to be seen by him as an interrogator rather than a helpmate or a friend. Finding myself in a familiar dilemma, I decided to leave him to his silences and tuck away topics of potential controversy for some later date.

That's where we've been for the past couple of days, in an emotional deadlock. Maybe marriage only has so much shelf life. In the early years, we gained strength from admitting our problems and working through them. But over the years we've tended to bury our troubles rather than face up to them. Having difficulties began to be seen as a sign of weakness or, worse still, failure. But today I yearn to get out from under all this repression.

Just now I have the desire to march up to our bedroom and shout: "Attention, please! Your presence is required here and now!" After all, I'm only responsible for half the attitude of this couple. I didn't reunite with this man after a year of dialoguing with myself to stay isolated and removed. I used to tell our two sons that they'd know they were truly in love if they never ran out of things to talk about with their intended mates, and I've always measured the depth of my connections by thoughts shared. The truth is that I love words — indeed, need words. Unsaid thoughts and withheld gestures make me panic. But, alas, I don't think Robin has ever felt responsible for sustained conversation, and as far as I can tell he appears to have as little fear of silence now as before. Pitiful or not, every action I have taken since his return has been linked to my need for meaning and connection. Our lack of intimacy seems to correspond directly to how much touching and talking we don't do. We have yet to see each other naked, and he tends to pat the kitten more than me.

We did have an odd meeting of sorts the other day when the cellar began to flood. Robin was puttering about in his new basement office when rainwater began seeping under the foundation during a daylong downpour. Dozens of towels placed near the door and exterior walls failed to absorb the lake that rose up outside the window. "Help! I need you right now," he shrieked in a way that brought me running to his aid, fearing that he might be having a heart attack. I found him cloaked in his slicker, a shovel in one hand and a push broom in the other.

"We've got to redirect the water," he said and motioned for me to follow him out into the elements.

We began sloshing about, Robin furiously digging a trench while I shoved the water down a nearby embankment. After ten minutes or so, mission accomplished, we collapsed inside the door, peeling wet clothes off of each other and feeling like saviors of our domain. Aside from nurturing the kitten, this was our first joint endeavor. The drama of it gave me a bit of a rush.

As I blew my hair dry and then put a kettle on for some tea, I realized that such moments are the building blocks of relationships. Trauma, problem solving, crisis — all those dark spots that we try to avoid — may be just what relationships need to keep them bubbling along. It occurs to me that we spend most of our lives learning how to avoid difficulty in order to project an image of confidence and success, thus losing the chance to expose our vulnerable selves, one to another.

At this point, I need to shake things up a bit — to take a reading on our location. Not unlike the captain of a ship who finds himself in the doldrums and needs to move his vessel along, I suddenly have the urge to find a way out of this deadlock we're in. I was never one to let the boys or Robin loll around for more than twenty-four hours, even when they had a bad case of the flu, and I'm not about to put up with it now. I mount the stairs, enter the bedroom, and in my most controlled voice ask Robin if there is anything I can do to lift his desolate mood. He shakes his head without uttering a single word. That response leaves me with two choices — attack or retreat yet again. I decide to plunge in like a faithful cheerleader, screaming her almost defeated team back to victory.

"Look," I blurt, not measuring my words now, "holing up, being antisocial, grasping for random straws is not going to cut it. We dull our lives by the way we conceive them."

"Seems to me we dull our lives when we put ourselves in a vast wasteland," he says. "Wasn't it your grandfather who described this place as nothing more than a sandy strip covered with scrub pine?"

Aghast, I remind myself to be patient. "But I thought you always loved the Cape."

"That was before I knew that most of its year-round inhabitants were octogenarians," Robin answers with a sneer.

"Oh c'mon, what are you talking about?"

"You should see them at the golf course," he continues, "mostly cranky and into their routine. Day in and day out they do the same thing, wear the same clothes, and when they're done playing, they complain about going home to the missus."

"There's life beyond the golf course, you know," I suggest.

"Well, if that's so, I don't see it. I wasn't aware that I was working all those years to end up changing furnace filters, doing the laundry, going to the market, and being a general handyman. In any case, golf gets me out of the house and out of your hair. Do you know how hard it is to watch you go about your business, together somehow, having a sense of purpose, in a way I never will?"

This is an unexpected turn. He envies my seemingly focused existence compared with his strangely circular one.

"You say I'm not finished," Robin continues. I feel my shoulders relax just a bit as he is obviously trying to stall the conversation, not wanting it to end.

"Of course you're not finished," I exclaim. "We're only halfway to a hundred. Use this place. The Cape holds secrets and answers that you haven't even begun to explore."

"Well, I did go off for an interview at the community college, and then there was the Arts' Council job. I thought I did well in both situations, but if they had been interested they would have called back weeks ago. There's no place for someone my age to grow out here."

"No comment," I say, sensing that we are moving into rough waters again. My spirit plunges into temporary darkness. I turn my back and head for the dresser to fold laundry that has been stacked there for a week and find myself wishing that he would go back on Prozac, a drug prescribed to him years ago as an antidote meant to counteract the effects of another medication. I was grateful when he gave it up because it had turned him into a neutered cat — pleasant, dull, but with no libido. Just now that would be preferable to his current antagonism and negativity.

"I hear you . . . I know there's more," Robin says, picking up on my dismay, his voice choking now. I can tell that he is holding back tears he doesn't want me to see. "I was reading through a brochure on international living," he continues, sounding momentarily upbeat, "and there are great opportunities for volunteer work in Vietnam and India. One thing that still turns me on is an adventure, like Africa. What do you think?"

What do I think? I mutter to myself. I think he's crazy, that's what I think! Traveling to exotic places is one thing — an extended stay at our stage of life is quite another! But he's always reached for grand schemes when he faces a dead end. I've learned not to react; instead I nod my head and hope that more explanation is forth-coming. Today he seems to have no encore, so I leave to take the dirty dishes to the kitchen. Often, detachment yields the greatest results.

Not one hour later Robin appears in the kitchen, cleaned up and ready to rejoin the human race. "What's up?" I ask nonchalantly, as if nothing has been unusual for the past seventy-two hours. He, the master at passive-aggressive behavior, has trained me well. Shutting up and shutting down, acting as if I don't really give a damn, usually works.

"I just remembered it's Thursday," he says, heading toward the cabinet under the kitchen sink where we keep the recycling containers, moving into action as he drags out the various bins of finished bottles and cans. I had almost forgotten that we had set aside Thursday for a dump run and beach walk — one activity designed to make us feel as though we are doing our civic duty, attempting to save this fragile land to which we've escaped for solace, and the other activity designed to invigorate. During moments such as these I find myself quoting my grandmother, who reminded us that "as the hands toil, so the spirit is raised above the troubled motions of the mind."

I'm eager for motion, anxious to get out of the house, and feeling momentarily liberated from the latest domestic stalemate. I grab my coat and happily load garbage bags, wine bottles, and empty soda cans into the trunk of the Volvo.

We take back roads, zigzagging on and off small lanes, not seeing a single other vehicle during the seven- to eight-minute ride. The stench from rotting garbage in the back is intense, and I'm eager to throw it away. In no time, we arrive at the garbage center, where we toss four or five green plastic bags into a chute and shove them down into a bottomless pit, never to be seen again. I wish it were that easy to push our own internal garbage away. Instead, for no definable reason, we hold on to it.

The next stop is the recycling area. Brightly painted signs tell us precisely where to deposit colored bottles, glass, batteries, newspapers, and other items. "I'll take the wine bottles," Robin suggests, hauling over a dozen empty chardonnays, merlots, and cabernets. I'm shocked by not only the amount we've consumed but also the drain such indulgence has on a budget. Are we getting through this initial period by softening the edges with booze, or is our evening ritual of fine wine and hearty food helping to pave our way back to one another?

We move on to the plastics and tin. As we follow the signs, taking care to get the right object in the right bin, I'm struck by the concentration it takes to recycle. Perhaps if we spent equal amounts of time recycling ourselves, we might resurrect something vital and new out of the old. It's an odd thought, especially since I'm having it at the dump, but it makes some sense. All this glass and plastic will be reduced to its original properties and then become something different. Wasn't I getting a glimpse of our original selves while reading the African letters? Have I been heading down the wrong path in thinking we needed to discover something that only needs recycling? That seems to be what last year was about for me. I didn't come here to reinvent myself. I simply returned to myself, to those original properties that had become dull with neglect or overuse. The same lessons should be applicable for relationships.

"Hey, don't just stand there," Robin yells from down the line of bins, bringing me out of my reverie and back to the task at hand. "Grab those newspapers and old magazines, would ya, sweetie," he says, animated and gregarious, a stark contrast from the withdrawn and vacant person of these past few days. I've come to believe that something as simple as getting out and taking action always counteracts a downward spiral. Thank God for garbage.

I hop back into the car and pull around to where Robin stands, anxious to head for the shore as the day is disappearing quickly. "Why don't we go to Forest Beach Road?" I suggest. "The channel walk is always invigorating, and from the looks of what's left of the sun, it's our best bet if we want to be home before dark."

"It's your call," he says, as I shift into first and head for a more alluring atmosphere. I flick on the radio, expecting my classical station, and instead hear the voice of Tina Turner belting out her fine rendition of "What's Love Got to Do with It?"

"Who's been messing with my radio?" I ask, even though I know the answer. His preference has always been for rock 'n' roll.

Just now, though, Tina's scratchy wail and raucous beat seem to be just what we need. I begin tapping the steering wheel with my fingertips, and he thumps the floorboard with his foot. I open the window and turn up the volume as we rattle across the mainland toward the ocean, both of us eager to let the air blow away three days of stifled emotions. I feel momentarily young again, remembering what it was like to jitterbug with this man who could move like no other. Robin interrupts my mood with a question.

"What *does* love have to do with it?"

"Excuse me?"

"What does love have to do with long-term marriage?"

I listen harder now to Tina's lyrics, trying to come up with an answer.

What's love got to do with it, got to do with it
What's love but a secondhand emotion.

"I don't know what love's got to do with it," I finally admit. "But I do remember some old chemistry that made us gel . . . that and a whole lot of hopeful projection about who I thought you were and vice versa."

He laughs with recognition at my hindsight. "I actually had an insight about marriage back at the dump," I continue.

"Joan, you are the only person I know who could find wisdom in garbage," he says, shaking his head in wonder.

Tina has given way to Whitney Houston singing "I Will Always Love You," from *The Bodyguard*. I loved that movie because it perpetuated the fantasy that there were men who would protect and defend their women.

"What did you come up with?"

I turn down the volume in order to continue the conversation.

"Well, there we were, methodically separating our plastic and tin and doing it because we knew that something new could be made out of the old stuff. Why not apply the same principle to us? Aren't we essentially the same people we once were? Our own original properties are buried in those of the marriage, not lost."

He ponders my thought as we pull into the beach parking lot and step out of the car, into the elements. But biting winds silence further conversation as we begin the mile-long trek to the channel. A good thing, actually, as my spirit always becomes one with the simplicity of the wide horizon, and for a time I am taken beyond myself, enjoying my solidarity with silence. I wonder if he derives as much pleasure from the scene as I do.

We pass a jetty that I recognize as the very

place a local photographer took our picture just before we left for Africa in 1963. "The mind does not erase," some poet once said, "and the soul cries out for the familiar." The local newspaper had wanted to do a story; Peace Corps volunteers made good copy. We posed in our bathing suits, sitting back to back, propped up against one another — two slim, tanned, carefree youths, unafraid and eager for a lifetime of adventures. In the way of lovers we were invincible, ready to replicate some of the various scenes played out by our parents and left for us to look at in the family photo albums.

Strange, that I should choose this beach upon which to walk. I wonder if Robin remembers, but I'm steeped in my own nostalgia and don't bother to ask him. Back then this place was made up of one long expanse. Gradually strong currents tore the coastline apart, and a series of breakers were added so that the sea would slap against the boulders rather than the fragile shore. It occurs to me that Robin and I didn't know to protect ourselves from the elements that would inevitably tear at our marriage. Still we walk here today, albeit less grounded, but moving in tandem nonetheless.

I spot a well-dressed young couple. She has long, straight blond hair; he looks like he just stepped out of a Ralph Lauren ad. Their appearance belies the discontent we hear — there are sharp words, but we cannot make out the context. She runs away from him, and he threatens to follow. I'm embarrassed that I'm witnessing their scene, but in a sick way I'm comforted by the reality that even the young and beautiful have their times of trouble.

When finally we arrive at the channel, I see that the wind's hand has created towering mounds of sand in some places and deep crevices in others. We take cover in one of the hollows and sit peering out, feeling held and nurtured by this wildly natural place. Just now our silence feels good. After a time, life with another should not be about gazing at each other but instead looking outward together at the same sight.

"You've got a point," Robin says, his words carried on the wind, back toward my direction.

"About what?" I ask, having completely forgotten the thread of our conversation.

"Original properties: mine, yours, ours. They're still with us. Surely you're as full of piss and vinegar as you ever were, but I'm stymied about myself. What did I bring to the relationship that hasn't been left behind with my career?"

As I search my mind, trying to recall how I portrayed him in the African letters, I'm distracted by a passing sailboat gingerly navigating its way out of the channel.

"What a strange time of year for a sail," Robin says, "and to venture out so late in the day. They must like living on the edge."

I crane my head and glimpse two sailors, a

man and a woman, grappling with lines — she unfurling sails, he leaning way out over the hull while gripping the rudder. We watch their momentary tension and deft actions as they hoist the mainsail and then take off into the wind, their faces registering excitement, two souls at the mercy of both the elements and each other, obviously wanting the challenge of sailing on a rough day.

"You used to like the edge," I say. "When did you stop wanting to risk?"

"When I began to lose," he answers, not missing a beat, "and when the stakes got high. Even so, I suppose I miss the rush." He wears a wayward expression.

"What is it?" I ask. "You're remembering something, aren't you?"

He nods his head. "When I crewed for my old prep school chum, Geoff, in the last race of the season. It was summer and warm, but overcast with high seas. I hated the tension, couldn't stand taking orders, was tense as hell as the boat took a real beating. But once we were over the finish line — I can't remember if we won or lost — I felt an exhilaration unlike anything I had ever felt before."

"Look," I blurt out, having held back most of my thoughts for the past few weeks, "it no longer matters what others think of us. Don't you suppose we could get back to risking, even though we might fail? Isn't that what drove us to Africa, to experience the unknown and be different?"

I pause to see if my passion is catching on and then continue.

"Seems to me, what you're aching for is obvious, and, what's more, it's yours for the taking. There's nothing stopping you from pursuing a dream or two. Didn't you tell the guys at your office that you were going off to live your unlived life? Listen, I know the future appears bleak, but please know your pleasure becomes mine. I've always loved you best when you've taken a dare or deviated from the path."

Robin doesn't pick up on my thoughts and that's all right. I don't want this moment to be cluttered with conversation. It's musing time. The sun has fallen into the sea, its faraway glow offering a colorful finale to a cloudy day.

We collect ourselves and head for the dune path, dawdling a bit as neither of us seems to want to retreat when the expanse of the outside offers such hope of possibility. A mere walk along the shore has exorcised the dreary state in which we found ourselves. Robin may revert back to his disenchantment; he may continue to protest retirement; he may never get the rush I do from this place. Even so, a day that began in the doldrums has lightened up; one that began with us apart has ended with us together.

4

Setting the Course

MID-NOVEMBER

The transitions of life's second half offer
a special kind of opportunity to break with
the social conditioning and do something
really new and different.

— William Bridges, *Transitions*

The kitchen counters are laden with ingredients for tonight's dinner party. It's Veterans Day weekend, and our summer friends who are here to close up their cottages are anxious to get together. I jumped at the chance to have them to dinner, thinking that mixed company would be a tonic for us just now. Although it took some convincing to bring Robin around to the idea of socializing, he didn't balk, for these are old friends with whom we share a twenty-five-year history. Regardless of how each of us has grown or diminished over the years, our summer get-togethers always feel like family reunions.

It was our children who discovered one another first as they caught tadpoles on the pond or played baseball in the street, but the parents quickly became intertwined. We had all sought summer refuge in a place where we could hide from the competitive world and be free of pretense for a time. Clambakes, sing-alongs, and charades provided the medicine for us during those summers gone by until, eventually, we found ourselves attending the weddings and baptisms of our children, the funerals of our parents, and epic birthdays, as we saw fit. Over time we began to touch the very root of each other's being. I suppose that's why it feels good to be fussing today.

I've settled on a mostly Down East theme: littlenecks in garlic butter will be an hors d'oeuvre, with a first course of stuffed artichokes. The entrée is coquilles St. Jacques, because bay scallops are in season, with anadama rolls, endive and grapefruit salad tossed with cranberries, and an apple pie for dessert. I've made a dramatic centerpiece for the dining room table of bittersweet and small cat-o'-nine-tails and collected beach rocks to use as place cards.

As the afternoon's light begins to fail, I step out into the chilly dusk to enjoy a moment of quiet with Robin, who has been chopping and stacking wood for the past couple of hours.

"Well, are you all set?" he asks, after watching me stir, stuff, chop, and knead various dishes most of the day, completely losing myself in the adventure of cooking.

"Almost. I really do get carried away! Must be because it's been so long since we've entertained."

"I'm glad you're having fun," he says, pleased with my domesticity. I even detect a note of relief in his voice, probably because it feels as though he has his old wife back. Besides, planning a party takes the focus off of our situation.

"Do you have any scoop on the gang since we last saw them?"

"Let's see . . . Woody and Paige have been on a cruise. No doubt they will talk about how wonderful it was; nothing they ever do seems to fall short of spectacular." He chuckles at my sarcasm. "I've no idea what's happening to Vince and Angie since he's left his job at the university. I suppose he's circulating his résumé, but who's looking for a dean when school is already in session? Hank and Carol are in therapy again with the same old issues — he's not getting enough sex, she wants him to express his feelings. That's about it. Oh, except for Lowell and Midge — they should be grandparents by now. Knowing her, they'll bring pictures."

"Should be a decent evening," Robin says, although I sense he is trying to brace himself for party chatter — not his favorite form of communication.

"I'm sure it will," I answer, knowing that something of summer always lingers around our time together. "At least we know that no one is any worse or better than we are," I continue.

"They never are," he says.

"I imagine they'll be curious as to how we're doing back together and partially retired," I offer. He shrugs, indicating that he's not bothered one way or the other. "Well, I'm off to take a bath. Don't forget to lay the fire and uncork the red wine," I say, tossing instructions over my shoulder.

Once in the tub, I sink under the bubbles and lean my head against the tile wall, letting the warmth of the water slow me down. Entertaining always gets my adrenaline pumping. It reminds me of our theater training back at Yale Drama School — all the hours of preparation are like the rehearsal, and then, when the first guest arrives, it's as if the curtain has lifted and the drama unfolds.

I'm especially hungry for girl talk since I have yet to make a close friend here. It takes only one woman to toss a confession into the ring for the others to follow suit. Last summer it was Carol who let slip that she'd had a dalliance with an old beau at her college reunion. Her revelations prompted a discussion about sex and the lack thereof. Even with Angie's new figure and Midge's eye tuck, no one was reporting a resurgence in their sensual lives. I wonder if we should take our lead from the French, who report that separate bedrooms as well as separate vacations do much to enhance marital romance.

I add more hot water and sink deeper into the tub. We almost never hear the men speak their truth. Although I imagine they share surface problems among themselves on the golf course, they rarely indicate problems or unhappiness in mixed company, so conditioned are they to deny any sort of strain — marital as well as professional. Carol occasionally gets them to open up. She's frequented so many psychics and shrinks that she has no fear of trying to lift everyone's armor. I wonder how the men will behave toward me — threatened or friendly. I haven't seen much of them since I broke the rules and balked at being a wife. Vince, who is old-world and Italian, is sure to attack me one way or another as he usually does. I don't think he has recovered from the fact that his prep school opened its doors to women ten years ago, and he continues to try to roll back the clock. Lowell, a Harvard-educated attorney, will entertain us as usual with his worldly cynicism, all the while staying emotionally removed. As for Hank, who now has more money than God since his search firm went public, he comes to these parties for diversion, not really caring what transpires, as long as the red wine flows abundantly.

I glance at my watch. They'll be here in ten minutes. I frantically scrub my legs and arms with a luscious bar of avocado soap and then slide under for one last soak. As I reach for a towel and step out of the tub, there's a knock at the door. Someone's arrived! I throw on a robe and rush out. Of course it's Woody and Paige — standard behavior for them to be early as they love parties and have a crowded calendar to prove it.

"Oh my goodness," Paige effuses in her oblique way, "you did say six, didn't you? I should have remembered that you're always running a bit late. Tell me what needs doing."

I point to the salmon dip and crackers, to be arranged on a platter as well as some mixed hors d'oeuvres and then retreat to the bedroom, feeling suddenly the slouch next to Paige. She recently hired a personal trainer and always appears, even at cocktail parties, with her ever-present bottle of water. I've never actually seen her without makeup, and tonight she is impeccable, dressed in a sleek beige and brown ensemble that complements her long, streaked hair.

"Oh dear," I say aloud while flipping through my limited wardrobe for something more flattering than my dark blue skirt and sweater set. But alas, I haven't shopped for over a year. My usual rags will have to do. I grab Robin and we stride out into the crowd, which has now swelled to Midge, Lowell, Vince, and Angie.

"It's summer rules," Robin announces, pointing to the bar that he's set up on the kitchen counter. "Everyone make their own." I pour myself a glass of chardonnay, pop the littlenecks in the oven, and lean back against the counter to observe the familiar shenanigans with amused affection. Twenty years ago, we all had such high hopes. We'd make big money, run large corporations, raise successful children, and live to brag about it all. Now, flawed and fallible, having attained much less than any of us silently hoped, we put our best face forward and try to erase the failures as we deceive ourselves in order to avoid our own realities. Somehow, we are beginning to look and sound like our dead parents.

Just then the last of the crowd appears —

Hank and Carol, all flushed and relaxed, having made it no secret that one way they're attempting to stay connected is by having regular Saturday sex. They arrive bearing wine and a gift for the garden — a slab of gray stone with a French phrase etched on its surface: L'AMOUR GRANDIT ICI.

"What does it say?" I ask Carol. "Can you translate?"

"Love grows here," she answers, dipping her chin and giving me a furtive look. I know she's more than curious as to how my life is going with a husband back in tow. Paige takes me off the hook, already into the details of their fabulous cruise. "We called at divine ports so undiscovered that no one had ever heard of them and *soooo* exclusive that we could swim nude in the light of day on deserted beaches. We haven't had such romance in years, if you know what I mean," she says, glowing with unparalleled sweetness, all the while glancing at Woody, who basks in her boasting as if it were all about his prowess. I am immediately sickened by, if not a little envious of, their lack of subtlety.

Fortunately Midge, whose newly shaped almond eyes have been everyone's initial focus, moves the talk from sex to babies. "After fourteen hours they decided on a C-section," she says, detailing her daughter-in-law's recent labor. "Look at this adorable little girl we've gotten! Having been spared the trauma of the birth canal, she has a perfectly shaped head," Midge gushes, all the while passing around a stack of up-close-and-personal shots direct from the delivery room — scenes only a mother would want to see — which send the men back to the martini pitcher and me to the oven to check on the stuffed artichokes. After all these years, we still can't stifle the urge to one-up each other, now and again. I yearn for the day when their myths collapse, as have ours, and we can finally interact with less pretension.

After one more round of drinks, I announce dinner. There is a shift of intensity as we move to the table — a doggedness in the conversation as each finds their bearings for the second act. We take our places and begin deflowering the artichokes. Vince immediately offers his to any taker, declaring, in his inimitable way, that artichokes are WASP food. His wife, embarrassed as usual by his brashness, gives him a cold stare, which the rest of us pretend not to notice. Dear Hank, always the social worker, mercifully intrudes on the awkwardness of the moment by reaching for our hands and suggesting grace. I'm surprised at his initiative since we don't usually bring God to these parties, but bow my head nonetheless, as Hank intones, "Heavenly Father, thank you for this preliminary thanksgiving and the gratitude we feel for old friendships celebrated here tonight. May we enjoy the harmony of togetherness and the grace of your blessings. Amen."

Vince pops up a second or two later and lifts his goblet. "Friendship, the wine of life, like a well-stocked cellar, should thus be constantly renewed. I love you guys," he says, as we clink glasses and go back to the artichokes.

"How many meals have we had at this table, anyway?" Vince asks.

"Who knows," Carol sighs, "but I wish I had kept a diary so it wasn't all such a blur."

"Well, if you had, we could have written a book, that's for sure," Vince says. "*On Peyton Pond*, that's what we'd call it!"

"Don't you wish," Hank chimes in. "Affable we've been, but hardly naughty."

"Just wild," Carol continues. "Remember the night of dirty charades?"

"And the greased watermelon contest in the pond," I recall, "where my supposedly noncompetitive husband wanted so badly for his team to win that he tore my bathing suit off as he grabbed the melon out of my arms."

"All in good fun, dear," Robin says, patting my knee.

"I'm not so sure," I answer, "but after all these years, who cares?"

"You two seem to be getting on pretty well," Carol says, her penetrating gaze aimed straight at Robin and me. "So, how's it going?"

I glance at Robin, whose eyes don't register a willingness to answer, and plunge in for the sake of getting the conversation going. "We're adjusting to each other's stubborn natures and idiosyncrasies," I answer, hoping to offer truth tinged with a bit of humor. "I can't deny the fact that it's a challenge." I pause. He still doesn't pick up the slack. "There's a lot to do here," I continue, sounding like a Welcome Wagon hostess. "You just have to find it. The most important thing is that the environment appeals to us. Right, honey?"

"Joan might wax poetic about the Cape's bucolic nature," Robin finally joins in, "and this place may have filled the soul of Thoreau, but I'm not sure what it's going to do for me."

His frankness leaves the table mute. They may not be ready to come here permanently, but they've all invested in the Cape and hold it up as a delicious dream. "I've sat in on a few planning board meetings, and I'm disgusted," Robin continues in his most cranky fashion. "No matter how hard they try to keep out the developers, they're buying their way in. Haven't you noticed all the new roads and chopped-up forests?"

"No kidding," Paige pipes up. "I detest what's happening — all the little hand-carved signs describing rows of houses — Somerset Woods, Cranberry Knoll. . . . It's awful. Where are all the old rose-covered cottages and picket fences?"

"Now, sweetie," Woody argues, gently rubbing his hand over her shoulders. "You're exaggerating. The old Cape still outweighs the new stuff."

"But not for long, Woody," Robin continues. "People don't mind commuting to Boston anymore. We'll soon be a bedroom community."

"Well, then there'll be more work opportunities for you," Hank inserts, both his tone and his statement meant to suggest that Robin was certainly too young to retire. "Surely you're not ready to throw in the towel, are you?"

"Not really, but the clock is ticking. If I'm going to do something, it'll have to be soon."

"In the meantime, how does it feel to be idle?" Vince asks, sounding truly curious now that he finds himself jobless.

"Yeah," Hank chimes in, "I can't imagine having nothing but leisure time on my hands."

"I can't imagine it either," Carol says, rolling her eyes. "Don't get any ideas. Not only do I like your money, but having you home all day would drive me crazy."

"C'mon, Carol, that was mean," Lowell says.

"Perhaps, but it's the truth. When he doesn't work or when the deals aren't coming in, he's a bear. Of course, his anger and intensity have been tempered now that we're in therapy, but still, what would we do with each other all day?"

I love her honesty. There are others around this table who surely see a shrink now and again, but they'd never come right out and admit it. I love Carol for throwing out her flagrant remarks . . . sex, children's mistakes, Hank's poor investments, and her own insecurities . . . you name it and she is willing to share it.

"Why thank you for acknowledging that I've reformed my behavior, dear," Hank says, blowing her a kiss while holding up his empty wineglass so she will refill it.

Robin has sat back in his chair, relieved that the focus is off him, just as Vince offers a suggestion. "You've always got the bank stock to fall back on," he says, his liquid memory now loosened by alcohol. "You could get on-line and become a day trader, using your stock as collateral. You're one of the lucky ones with family money," he says, a tinge of envy in his slight smile.

"I'm not that flush," Robin retorts, annoyed that our financial situation has been put on the table. "Besides, even though money is an issue, I also have a gnawing sense that I need to go deeper," he says, unexpectedly taking this practical conversation to a more philosophical level.

"Deeper?" Hank asks. "Where is deeper?"

"If it's the volunteer world you're talking about, who can afford that?" Woody asks.

I clear the salad plates and run the scallops under the broiler. Their probing is making me antsy, and I'm annoyed that success always seems to come down to material security and advantages. I hate the way that people are identified only by what they do, not by who they are. As I present the sizzling entrée, I'm still trying to assemble my scattered senses, knowing that what I am about to say will incite Vince. "There's more to living than money and the next deal," I say.

"Who asked you?" Vince scolds, diminishing my point as irrelevant and gulping what remains of his pinot noir. "Your husband's future is the

76

subject of our conversation. Oh man, Joan," he sighs, glancing reproachfully at me, "ever since I've known you, you always tried to steal his light."

That stings. Vince and I frequently have words, but rarely does it get this harsh. "I beg your pardon," I fire back. "I'm living with this man. Even though I'm not messing with his future, I've got my preferences. I'd love to see him involved in social services or something cause-oriented, where he can feel that his work reflects his values. He hasn't had that since Africa."

"You're not getting touchy-feely on me, are you?" Vince chides, as usual steering clear of emotional issues.

"Not really," I answer, and then go for the jugular. "What would you know of feelings anyway?"

We're off and running. Robin opens another bottle of wine, which Hank quickly grasps in order to fill up his own glass before pouring another round.

"Vince, I thought you weren't going to get on Joan's case anymore," Angie says, coming to attention, being unusually confrontational for a change. "You always manage to bring the conversation to a new low," she adds.

"It's all right, Angie," I reassure her. "A little tension isn't going to kill me."

Vince settles back into his chair, but only for a moment. "What I've been wanting to tell you ever since you dropped your married name and went back to Anderson is that you've changed somehow, and not for the better."

"Well, thanks for your unsolicited opinion," I say. "Would you believe that my decision had to do with money?"

"No, I certainly would not," he says, radiating control, waiting for more of an explanation.

"Well, guess what? Once I found out that reviewers, bookstores, and libraries arrange nonfiction books in alphabetical order by the author's last name, I changed back from W to A. It seemed to make good business sense; you'd have changed, too."

"Hell, it doesn't bother me," Robin quips, amused now that the conversation is turning sexist. "I just say, show me the money."

"It's still insulting," Vince continues, holding fast to his opinion.

"Oh, come off it, Vince," Lowell chimes in. "When it's about money, you always go for it."

"And who says Robin's been insulted?" Angie asks. "Perhaps he's perfectly happy with this arrangement. After all, if Joan writes something compromising or embarrassing, he doesn't have to live with shame by association."

"I've kept my maiden name at school," Midge adds. "When we married, it was too confusing for the first graders to think of me as anyone but Miss Shafer. Besides, it makes me feel connected to my roots — particularly my dad. You're just trying to get our backs up again, Vince."

"OK," he concedes, "but I would object to a wife getting rid of my name for just about any other reason."

"That's because you're so patriarchal," Carol inserts. "The whole tradition of women exchanging their father's names for their husband's is one more example of how one sex is keeping the other under wraps."

"You know, I sense what the women are talking about," Robin chimes in. "Hell, I've been a slave to the patriarchy my whole life."

"Oh, c'mon," Vince says. "Are you becoming a clone of your feminist wife?"

"Watch it, Vince," Robin cautions. "The whole damn world has been designed by patriarchal principles . . . you should know that. Academia is one of the worst offenders. Their pecking order is ruthless. Only so many professors are granted tenure, and as for deanships, well, that's a closed club. The same holds true for law, medicine, even the church. They're all designed with just so much room at the top. Now that I'm out of the institutional loop I'm beginning to get an inkling of what it's like to be my own man."

Hmm, I muse. His thinking seems to be shifting. I had noticed that his reading had changed from Robin Cook and Tom Clancy to heavier stuff by Thomas Merton, Carl Jung, and M. Scott Peck.

"It's a shock, sure," Robin continues, "when all of a sudden one's days are without structure and focus. But, for the first time since I was sixteen, I'm about to captain my own ship, even though I'm uncertain as to where I'm headed."

"I can understand that," Vince says, stifling a yawn, "especially the part about structure and focus. Without a goal, I'm lost." Bombastic a moment ago, Vince is typically meek the next. At this late hour, however, no one picks up on his somber note. Retirement talk is one thing; unemployment is quite another.

I begin to clear the dishes to make room for apple pie and hopefully some lighter conversation. We're heading into the third act with snifters of brandy and an unspoken moratorium on intensity. Through fatigue and suppressed yawns, the conversation winds down.

"We've lost Hank," Carol says, just as his eyes close and his head begins bobbing. "C'mon, Hank, time to go bye-bye." He startles, offers a lazy smile, and lets Carol help him up and into his coat. "Save me some pie, please. We'll see you before we leave on Monday."

I hope the others will detect my weary look and take their leave as well, but instead they move toward more comfortable chairs in the living room. Paige and Woody grab the couch and immediately entangle themselves; she rests her head on his shoulder and purrs like a cat, while he twirls her hair. Must they always be so purposefully demonstrative? The floor and odd chairs are left to the rest of us.

"Carol sure was her old salty self," Lowell says.

"Yeah, but all that therapy is changing her," Vince is quick to point out. "Didn't you notice her edginess and how she put down Hank right in front of us? That's new behavior, and as far as I'm concerned, it always appears when some shrink is encouraging the couple to be honest with one another."

"Not a bad idea," I chirp. "When you drop the mask, life becomes real — not a bad place to be at our stage of the game. At least Carol has placed her wants and needs on the table."

My thoughts go unanswered, and now Angie is making moves toward the coat closet.

"Look," Robin interjects, "we're all just muddling through."

"Limping is a better word," Angie says, tossing her truth over her shoulder.

"Whatever," Robin continues, "but at least we're demonstrating staying power."

"I'll give you that," Vince says, finally agreeing to something.

I'm beginning to wish that each of us could find some manner of temporary resolution for the dilemmas we find ourselves in: that someone or some institution would find my husband and pluck him out of his confusion; that Vince would once again find a home in some university where his brilliance would truly be appreciated; that Woody and Paige could learn that we would love them better if they weren't so picture-perfect; that Lowell might stop being chief counsel and come down to our level once in a while. It should be getting easier to share our fallibilities and look at one another as if in a mirror, in order to laugh at who we haven't become.

Even so, the evening has offered the diversion I sought, as well as the reminder that every time we gather nuggets of ideas are offered for me to mull over. Most interesting tonight was Robin's new tack — away from his conservative leanings toward more androgynous thinking.

After hugs and large gestures of half-drunken goodwill, they're gone. I close the door and lean against it, knowing that such intensity and downright drama will not be ours again for some time. As Robin begins to tackle the mountain of greasy soup bowls and silverware, I change into my unlovely but comfortable flannel nightgown and then collect stray glasses and dessert plates.

"They do drink martinis like water," he says, holding up the empty Absolut bottle before flinging it into the recycling bin. I grab a dish towel and begin drying the glassware. "You certainly surprised me tonight," I say.

He smiles and continues to scrub the copper bottoms of the pots and pans with steel wool. With a wistful tone in his voice, he makes a confession: "I wish I felt old. Then I wouldn't have so many young thoughts."

"That's both profound and painful. If you felt old, you wouldn't bother trying to grow anymore. But that's not the case, right?"

"You've got it. But I'm still frustrated and impatient that I can't figure out where I should be headed."

"At least you're confronting the questions. Some of the world's most famous men and women only came to do their great deeds in the second half of their lives."

"Oh yeah? Like who?"

"Gandhi, Gauguin, Grandma Moses, Jimmy Carter . . ."

"That's inspiring," he says while letting the water out of the drain. "It was quite an evening. Although Vince was pretty hard on you."

"I know, but this time he couldn't help himself. Couldn't you feel his frustration . . . his utter lack of control? Out of all of you guys, I thought his job was the most secure. He's been at Parsons forever. Has he even hinted to you guys what happened?" I ask, curious about the real story.

"Not really. But I think it's no more complicated than the college got a new president — a woman no less — and obviously their personalities clashed. It's a shame he can't open up and tell us the story. What a waste pride is," he says with a shake of his head.

"Remember that summer about ten years ago when you were down on yourself," I remind him, "and we never socialized with anyone?"

"I guess so," he admits.

"It wasn't until years later that we owned up to our trouble. Vince thought then that our avoidance had something to do with him," I say. "Silence is so often misinterpreted."

"You'd think he'd remember that now," Robin says, while taking a last swig of brandy out of someone's glass. "Everyone in the gang has had their series of downfalls and challenges."

"I used to think that being an attorney or having your Ph.D. guaranteed your future — that once you endured all the education and practice, you'd be assured of a smoother ride. What's happened to Vince only points up that there are no guarantees," I say.

"So, after all these years, you no longer regret not marrying that guy from Yale Law?" Robin teases.

"God, no," I say with sarcastic humor. "It's much more amusing to be with someone whose life is unpredictable," I say, rolling my eyes.

We laugh at my folly as I blow out the candles while my mind flashes to my father's funeral, when I realized that no one knew what he had done for a living. What's more, no one cared — they just loved the man for his generosity of spirit. That's what brought hundreds of people to his service. I should have known then and there that material accomplishments are rarely a true reflection of who we are.

"What Vince doesn't know is that he hasn't lost everything," I say. "He does have himself, after all."

"Time for bed," Robin says, putting his arm around my shoulders and guiding me toward the stairs. We hoist our weary bodies up to the loft, which tonight feels like a warm nest, and fall into a long, silent hug, no longer stranded from one another. I sense a team is being reconfigured, and it feels good. I wonder what the others are saying about us behind closed doors.

5

The Wind at My Back

EARLY DECEMBER

Reach for the fullness of human life — If you but touch it, it will fascinate. We live it all, but few live it knowingly.

— Goethe, *Faust*

I am barreling down the Mid-Cape Highway on a cold winter's morning, bolting for a short time from domestic rigors, taking flight like the gull that is trailing my car. Alone in my Volvo, sipping a cup of hazelnut coffee, with classical guitar music stirring my senses, I am momentarily regaining myself, that wild and free woman I learned to become last year. A bright orange ball of sun is rising over the ocean behind me, tinting the patches of snow alongside the highway pink. As a strong wind buffets the car and I tighten my grasp on the steering wheel, I'm propelled by the energy of adventure.

The excuse for getting away appeared quite suddenly. A favorite magazine editor called to ask if I'd have time to do a profile of a female racewalker who is now in training for the Olympics. "She's thirty-something," he said, "married with two children — only took up the sport a couple of years ago, and works her training sessions in and around her family's needs — a real enigma. I need a woman writer, someone who will look for the behind-the-scenes conflicts and demons that make her quest all the more awe-inspiring."

Immediately I was tempted. I loved the idea of stepping in to observe the life of someone who was pushing the limit. Besides, I can never afford to reject unsolicited assignments, so I accepted eagerly. Now, with each passing mile I am fueled by the impending challenge — it's as if a gust of wind has swept me up and I'm mad to go in its direction. I love it when outside forces conspire to send me into new realms.

At first Robin welcomed my opportunity, especially the prospect of extra income. Abruptly, though, he changed his tone. "What's the urgency?" he wondered. "With Christmas around the corner and some of our kids coming home, couldn't you put off the meeting until January? For God's sake, Joan, from the glint in your eye, I feel as though you're just dying to get away from me."

He was right, of course. I did have several months to accomplish the task, so why was I determined to go now? To get away for a few days, that's all — to be off-duty from relationship. But I didn't tell him that.

"It's true, I'm excited to meet this woman," I said, hoping to cover up the anticipation I felt about the prospect of being alone. "Her discipline intrigues me — and the fact that she is pursuing a dream even though she has a family to think about."

"I guess I wouldn't feel quite so threatened," he admitted, "if you hadn't taken yourself away last year. Perhaps I fear that one of these times you'll just keep going!" I could take his remark as a compliment — that he doesn't want me out of his sight because he loves me so much — but I'm too shrewd for that. I sensed he simply feared being alone, left in an empty house with only himself for company. My mind flashed to a sentiment by Somerset Maugham: "A woman will always sacrifice herself if you give her the opportunity." "You know," I said cheerily, "I've read that men in some primitive tribes send their women away five and six times a year to refresh their intuition and instincts. Not a bad idea, considering how burned out most American women are. Besides, I always come back from these trips ebullient and refreshed, with more tales than even you care to hear about."

Despite my campaigning for the efficacy of short separations, Robin stood in the kitchen on the day of departure looking like a wounded puppy as I slapped ham and cheese between two slices of bread for my brown-bag lunch, all the while willing myself not to feel so conflicted. I continue to be a sucker for his guilt trips. Both the training by my mother and my own years of parenting make it hard for me to let go of the impulse to nurture.

"Don't take it so personally, honey," I said on my way to collect my notebook and briefcase. "It's my job, after all. I've left a tuna noodle casserole in the fridge, and there's beef stew cooking in the Crock-Pot." Without so much as a thank-you, he refilled his coffee mug.

I actually understand his testiness and envy. Not only am I getting away, but I have a project to tackle. He has neither just now and that must hurt. He has forgotten all the business trips in his past, when he floated from one educational seminar to another, delivering papers, stimulating his mind, massaging his ego, while I was at home with the children. Will it always be such a struggle to embrace the opportunities I know I deserve if they don't include him? Will I always feel as though warring nations exist within me?

I suppose so, unless of course some miracle occurs that offers him a challenge. In the meantime, I will continue the extra caretaking that is meant to show concern. If truth were told, however, these gestures are often nothing more than a bribe, as if I'm pleading, *Please see the tuna casserole as a token of my love,* even though I'm getting my way and running off. There's no doubt that retirement slows men down just as motherhood slows women down. Why can't our periods of intensity and power be more in sync?

I shake my head to rid myself of further guilt as I clear the Sagamore Bridge and head up the highway toward Boston. I'm filled with a sense of possibility, even a tinge of invincibility, important ingredients for the creation of evolving selfhood. At least that's what Joan Erikson, my ninety-two-year-old mentor, was always espousing. "Get out and actualize your potential," she would urge. "Create something out of nothing. That's where the joy is." Her philosophy, which I always carry with me, comes in handy when I question my actions. I shake my head, amazed at how much she encouraged my wild side. "They want to tame you, dear," she would say with a twinkle, "but you need to keep fighting to be an individual." Joan would approve of this trip. I can feel her cheering me on. She was forever running away and breaking the rules, reveling in her independence, eager to learn any skill that would offer escape.

I slap the steering wheel as if to say yes, sink back into the seat, sip what remains of my coffee, and press my foot on the accelerator. "It's important not to deny the self in order to please others," Joan would tell me. "You'll only lose your self in the process." This is not about running away, it is about running forward. As the road winds inland, I yield to the new landscape of towering trees and rolling hills and become an adventurous nomad, welcoming whatever comes next.

In time I clear Boston and drive on, feeling seasonal with Celtic harp music playing on the radio, snowflakes dancing on the windows, and Eriksonian wisdom whirling around in my head. Suddenly a loud explosion and a grinding noise shock me out of my musings. The car veers to the right, then onto the sandy shoulder until it comes to an abrupt halt. My heart pounds as I carefully slide out the door, afraid to see the damage. I'm relieved when I see the front right tire, hopelessly flat, with a strip of rubber flapping in the wind.

I've changed tires in the past, I think defensively, no problem, and with that thought, I unload the necessary tools, line them up like a surgeon about to perform an operation, pop off the hubcap to tackle the lug nuts, then step on the tire wrench to apply the necessary pressure. Alas, they won't budge, not even one of them.

Suddenly I'm grateful that Robin placed his cell phone in my hand before I left home. Although I abhor the way they encourage us to lead such harried lives, just now I applaud their invention. I dial AAA road service, offer up my card number, and anticipate imminent rescue. "Your card has expired," a pleasant man at the other end informs me. "I can send a tow truck, but it'll cost you."

"How long before it gets here?" I shout above the noise of cars whizzing by. "My fingers are in the early stages of frostbite."

"Under an hour," he answers, and with that we're disconnected. No longer feeling tranquil, I crawl into the backseat of the car, huddle under my winter coat, and call my racewalker to tell her that I'll be late. Near the end of last year I found myself thinking that danger and solitude are two factors that go into forming one's character, but out here, in this alien atmosphere, I suddenly could care less about my character. I feel desperate, agitated, and angry with Robin for not taking care of the membership. I call home in hopes of getting some sympathy for my predicament.

"I didn't think you'd call so soon," he says, genuinely surprised and pleased to hear my voice. "Where are you?"

"In New Hampshire, on the side of the road. I've had a blowout."

"Are you all right?"

"Yes," I answer curtly.

"You did call AAA, didn't you?" he asks, offering the only solution he can from such a distance.

"Yep, but the card has expired. This is going to cost us," I say in a flat voice, hoping to make it clear that I'm not only inconvenienced but also annoyed. "I thought you'd paid the bill."

"I guess that's just one more thing I've let slip in all this transition. I'm really sorry, sweetie," he answers, sounding contrite. "I hope you aren't too cold. Are you safe?"

It's pitiful that his concern softens me. "I'm in a pine forest — lots of snow everywhere. At least it's not Boston."

"How long before the tow truck gets there?" he asks.

"Under an hour," I answer. "I have my lunch to eat, and I can always organize my notes. I'll call you when I'm on my way again."

"Take care," he says. "Don't get out of the car now, you hear?"

I press the power button to off and reflect on

my need to call home — a habit left over from earlier times before I learned that reaching for rescue rarely works. Rather, accepting my fate and then being quiet for a while offers more consolation — that and sitting in a winter-wrapped world.

Eventually the tow truck comes, the tire is changed, and I'm on my way again, following a flock of wild geese flying in the shape of a V. My focus shifts to athletes, Ann Dow in particular, and my preliminary phone conversation with her. She seems low-key, not at all egocentric, a Roman Catholic who leans strongly on her faith, and somewhat concerned that I will portray her as an ordinary person who races simply because she enjoys it. Since her sport is a lonely one that doesn't attract spectators, I suspect that her training is as much spiritual as it is physical, and that getting to know her will involve more observation than talk. I recall the same of Joan Erikson and the other active people I have known. Catch them if you can, they seem to say, welcoming outsiders to their world but teaching mostly by example.

By late afternoon I arrive at my destination, ring the doorbell, and promptly experience the adrenaline rush that comes from stepping into the unknown. Despite this woman's modesty on the phone, I'm daunted by her being an Olympic hopeful, expecting someone well sculpted and powerful. But my apprehension dissolves when she opens the door: There stands a freckle-faced girl-next-door type, clad in faded jeans and a sweatshirt. She greets me warmly, extending her hand and a firm grip as she ushers me into her world.

There is little evidence of athleticism anywhere, save for a basket full of well-worn running shoes, which sits in the hallway beneath a row of hooks that hold silk underwear, lightweight vests, and myriad warm-up suits. Nowhere is there training equipment or a weight room, both of which I expected to see. The only clue that this might be the home of a professional athlete is a poster on the wall that reads "Remember always that the will to win is nothing without the will to prepare."

We settle into the kitchen, where her son and daughter busy themselves with homework while Ann makes supper. Although I sense a smoldering energy under her unassuming body language, the scene is disarmingly normal, not nearly obsessive enough. After I spot several piles of dirty laundry and eavesdrop on five or six phone calls she receives from the church, school, and extended family, I finally ask: "How do you manage it all?"

"Stolen moments," she says. "I make the most of my time when the kids are at school. Besides that, I have a totally supportive husband." Her voice softens when she speaks of him. "He changed jobs so his hours would be more flexible," she continues, "and he was behind our move from the suburbs to town to shorten my carpooling. As a result I get another hour of training every day."

My mind wanders to the inflexibility of husbands I know who see their job as the more significant one.

"Was he always so unselfish?" I ask.

"Well, we didn't get married with this lifestyle in mind," she admits, laughing, "so we did have some psychological adjustments to make. But after I was spotted in a race by a well-known coach who encouraged me to take the sport more seriously, we were forced to consider what that would mean, not only to me but the entire family."

"The family," I countered, "how did you suppose racewalking would benefit them?"

"We've been to Disneyland twice," her daughter piped up, obviously eavesdropping on our conversation, "and last year Mom took me with her to Spain and France."

I find myself wondering if daughters are more tuned in to their mothers' lives than sons. Her son remains quiet, not unlike my boys, who still barely acknowledge that I am anything other than their mother.

"How else does it contribute to your kids' lives?" I continue to probe.

"We all have our individual roles in this family," she continues. "No one's job is more important than anyone else's."

"Except right now," her daughter inserts. "Nobody understands, that my mom is training for the Olympics," she says, sounding frustrated. "I had to explain to my teacher today that racewalking is your job, not just a hobby."

Obviously the children are intuiting their mother's values. By blending her aspirations with family responsibilities, she is modeling the ideal that each person needs to find an identity of their own. As if she has read my thoughts, Ann tells me that her mother always believed that the only way to be a good parent was to be a whole person. It occurs to me that the same principles apply to marriage — the only way to be a good spouse is to be a whole person as well.

We finish up our conversation over a home-cooked Mexican dinner and then arrange to meet at nine in the morning. Once in my motel room and alone with my thoughts, I am most struck by this woman's sense of calling — her certainty that she bears a uniqueness that is asking to be lived. Joan Erikson had a similar tenacity, and I sense that it is no accident that I should find myself face-to-face with another woman who values her autonomy and is driven by her gifts. Their common message is about living attentively, taking steps for self, and embracing their uniqueness with gusto.

Finally in bed, I drift into slumber, pleasantly surprised that what started out as an ordinary assignment is an opportunity for more learning — that and the realization that mentors can come from any age group.

Dressed in sweats and a warm sweater, fresh

from dropping the children off at school, Ann begins her day at a local gym with me tagging along. Here she stretches into a sweat, her face becoming flushed as she twists like a contortionist, before moving on to the weights. No frenetic hurry here — no shortcuts to victory. It's all about plodding along, making small gains, shaving off a second here or there, and gradually building one strength upon another. Today she'll follow up her long walk with yoga, which helps her with concentration. As she holds each yoga pose, she'll repeat her mantra: "I can do all things through God who makes me strong."

After several hours of her workout routine, she laces up her orange lightweight sneakers, and we're off for her long walk during which I hope to keep up with her. Until now, this glimpse into her life has been fascinating. But I am unnerved at the prospect of walking beside her. Nevertheless, I stuff my anxiety, hop into the car, and off we go to the outskirts of town, where a bike trail circumnavigates a lake. Ann starts slowly, no doubt in deference to me, but she gradually quickens her pace, and I am forced to jog in order to keep up. I try to stifle my heavy breathing so she won't detect how out of shape I really am. Rather than be embarrassed, why don't I do something about fitness?

Gradually my feet find a cadence that carries me along. Mercifully, we don't speak, which allows me to focus on her and mentally record my impressions. She checks her watch, adjusts her gait, and gradually increases her speed, all the while monitoring her breathing, posture, form, and pace. "I'm so lucky," she says, breaking into a smile, "having a job that forces me into the woods every day. Can you imagine anything better — working out and fine-tuning this old body of mine?"

"Doesn't look like an old body to me," I quip, feeling my fat jiggle under my sweatshirt and, unlike her, thinking of a hundred other things that I might enjoy better than incessant training.

"Yeah, well, if I make the Olympic team, I'll be one of the oldest athletes. The last time I was at the training center, it occurred to me that I could be somebody's mother."

"Do you live to walk or walk to live?" I ask through my huffing and puffing.

"Both," she says. "I can't imagine life without intense exercise. I've always needed the mental and physical challenge."

Just as we face an uphill grade of seemingly monstrous proportions, she thoughtfully suggests I veer off to the right and follow the lower path. "I'll meet up with you in forty-five minutes or so," she says, casually tossing her instructions over her shoulder. "Your landmark is an old green bench," and with that, she's out of sight.

I slow to a crawl and collapse on a boulder, catching my breath in order to merge with nature's conversation and drink in the simplicity of barren trees now dappled with last evening's snowfall. In time, I am serenaded by tree sparrows, their voices sounding like tiny wind chimes, which inspire me to get up and begin walking again. Strangely empowered by Ann's quest, I tell myself that it's never too late or too early to be what I need to be. Although my time has passed to become a serious athlete, I could still be athletic.

The wind picks up, and as I'm buoyed by a brief snow squall, so are my thoughts. I stick my tongue out to catch a few flakes and hear Joan Erikson's words: "It's a wonderful thing to be able to use your body," she would say. "When you rely on your body and honor its sensations, not just the muscles, but all its capabilities, you are never estranged from life."

My pace increases and I break into a jog. I'm feeling that runner's high that they talk about, and now I want to go beyond the point where Ann and I arranged to meet. As I plunge ahead, skimming over newly fallen snow, the words of my favorite poet, Derek Walcott, begin to make sense: "The time will come when, with elation, you will greet yourself arriving at your own door, in your own mirror, and each will smile at the other's welcome."

Alone and full of myself, I feel as though I could go on forever, no longer anxious for this part of my day to be over. I'm getting a glimmer of my racewalker's mentality and understanding a bit more about what drives her. It seems only a few minutes or so when Ann emerges out of nowhere. "Hey, how did you get here so fast?" she wonders.

"Your inspiration," I answer. "Trying, in my own way, to outdo myself, for a change. You've helped me retrench and gather up my waning energies."

She gives me a hug, pleased that she can be a motivating influence on someone else, and then we part — she to return to motherhood, me to meet her coach in Cambridge. I suspect that the details of her training and his opinions about her tenacity will not be the focus of this story.

Twenty-four hours later, I'm heading home. With a notebook full of impressions and a newly found resolve to never look back, always look forward, I shake my head, once again, at the confluence of events. Although in the past I've thought that only the elderly possessed wisdom, I now find that age has nothing to do with it. It's more about life experience — the hand that each of us is dealt and how we make the most of the destinies we inherit. Both Joan Erikson and Ann Dow are women who were made to be survivors early in their lives. Ann dove into a pool and drowned the sorrow she harbored over her parents' divorce in competitive swimming, while Joan Erikson ran away from a depressed mother and a straitlaced preacher father to study dance in Europe. Both relied on action to move them from sadness to success, instinctively understanding that only they could create their own fulfillment — no one was going to do it for them. There existed an urgency within them not to put their lives on hold but instead to reach for their dreams. It is both a gift and a burden to be driven to selfhood, but do any of us really have a choice?

Such are my thoughts as I drive over the Sagamore Bridge just as the sun is setting over the bay. It felt good to flee, but it feels equally good to be returning home. Curiously enough, both endeavors contain enticing elements of adventure. The trees lining the roadway stand dark and bare, yet the dome of indigo blue sky and a half moon help brighten my journey's end. The road is empty — no one is venturing out to the Cape at suppertime on a cold December night. Within the hour, the Volvo is creeping through the brush, up our sandy road, and, voilà, I'm back! The normally dark house has been illuminated. In every window there is an electric candle! I see Robin waving from the front porch as I pull my car beside his and hop out, leaving my duffel to be retrieved later, eager now for a hug.

"It's beautiful . . . the house, I mean. How did you know I have always wanted candles in the window?" He gives me another squeeze, not bothering to tell me how he read my mind. Inside, the welcoming smell of spaghetti sauce bubbling on the stove signals to me that this man has been busy.

"Since when did you learn to make tomato sauce?" I ask.

"It's store-bought," he says, while uncorking a bottle of Chianti. "But I did add onions, sausage, and pepper like I've seen you do. So, tell me, how was the trip?" He seems eager for news of the outside world.

"No, you go first," I say, remembering that once, when he returned from one of his conferences, he gave me the stage, wanting to hear what had transpired in our life rather than tooting his own horn. "From the looks of things, it seems you survived."

"More than that," he says, handing me a wineglass as we settle on chairs beside the old pine table. "Those first few hours felt so empty — reminiscent of last year and living alone, stuffing myself with cocktails and cookies. But right after your phone call I decided to take action and do something other than the long list of chores I had made for myself. I took off to the conservancy land, your stomping ground."

"Isn't it beautiful?" I said. "The colors and wildlife change, not just with every season, but practically every day."

"So many berries and birds," he said, shaking his head. "I can see why you go there," he continues. "Anyhow, just as I was rounding the bend . . . you know, where you make the turn into the meadow . . . there in front of me, lined up in a row as if at attention, was a pack of coyotes — ten or twelve of them. It was daunting."

I can barely picture what he is saying.

"They are huge animals, so powerful-looking,

even the pups," he continues. "I think the last time I came face-to-face with anything that wild was back in Uganda."

"Were you frightened?" I asked.

"All I felt was that they were in control. I wasn't sure what to do or where to go, so I simply froze in place."

"Then what?"

"A couple of seconds later they started wrestling with one another, obviously not interested in me any longer. I searched for an alternative route out of there, not wanting to intrude on their territory or turn my back on them. Came home along the bog," he said, his voice almost inaudible now, a man humbled by nature. "I haven't felt that vulnerable in years." Another pause. "I guess I was made to realize that there are powerful forces I can't control," he continues. "There's a big world around me . . . one that I've ignored for too long."

"How so?" I asked, not sure about the conclusions he is about to draw.

"We've all adapted so readily to the domesticated life," he continues, "staying inside for the most part, rarely embracing the wild and natural. It's time I begin to look inside myself and unleash that which is untamed."

Amazing, I think silently. Although the seals had a huge impact on me and gave focus to the repairing of my life last year, I never thought that Robin would be touched by wildness in a similar manner.

The way is never straight. Everywhere there is offhanded revelation. We're each responsible for collecting and registering our own unique moments, but at the end of the day, it helps to have someone with whom we can share our progress — someone who applauds not only the direction we take but also the origins of the journey. I feel a tingle in my spine. My journey away spawned his journey within. Excitement comes as we continually attend to the mysteries of who we are to become.

6

Buoyed

CHRISTMAS EVE

I do not think we can ever adequately define
or understand love; I do not think we were
ever meant to. We are meant to participate
in love without really comprehending it.
We are meant to live into love's mystery.

— Gerald May, *The Awakened Heart*

Alas, the best-made plans go askew. Just now a blizzard is paralyzing the eastern seaboard, and although I love the idea of a white Christmas, I'm hoping for a break in the accumulation so that our eldest son, Andrew, and his wife can get here. They were due in yesterday morning, then delayed until later that evening. Today, Christmas Eve, there was no sign of them until a few minutes ago when they called from the airplane to say they'd be in Providence by three.

I had planned for all four of us to decorate the tree, gather greens from the woods, and prepare some special foods, but those preparations have long since been accomplished. For the past day or two Robin and I have been left with nothing more than our anticipation tinged with a bit of anxiety. Getting along with married children requires much improvisation, and we're very much the amateurs in this, one of the most daunting of familial games. Since neither of our sons has made it home for the holidays since they've married, we're a bit out of practice as to how to do Christmas.

"Be Margaret Mead," a good friend suggested. "Observe, digest impressions, and while you're having the experience, be sure not to miss the meaning along the way."

Easy for her to say, I want to retort. She is the mother of three married daughters, two of whom are in and out of her life as if they'd never left home. I've grown to suspect that continuing a relationship with sons is more difficult as they tend to adopt their wives' expectations and attitudes much more swiftly. Although I've read that all types of closeness tend to become reduced as time goes on, I still find it difficult to be with sons who ever so gradually censor their behavior as well as their stories.

"I've been saying good-bye to my boys for years," a friend confessed the other day, "and it still isn't over. I didn't think it would be this way. The separation happened gradually. First they attached themselves to their favorite teacher, then to a trail of girlfriends, and finally their wives, who serve many of the purposes I used to have."

"I know," I admit. "But after having a say in most of their transitions, the big adjustment is not having a say at all. For me, a sort of role reversal has taken place. I'm feeling like the child learning to play in their game, and they are the parents, imparting all the instructions."

Although we've been relocated to supporting actors in their drama, I do want to fit into their new families somehow. It's not about control.

Rather, it's about having a perceived role other than in-law or grandmother. There are many illusions that I've fought for and then let go over the years, but I refuse to give up knowing my grown children. Although their quest for adulthood has long since commenced, and it certainly is healthy for them to rely on their inner voices rather than that of their parents, the result is that we only skim the surface of our mutual lives.

It wasn't that way before they were married. Then they came to visit and willingly participated in anything we happened to be doing. So enthralled was Andrew's bride, Shelly, by the warmth we created at their rehearsal dinner that she struggled to make sure Robin knew of her appreciation by standing on a chair, in order to look into his eyes and tell him how affirmed she felt. "If there was any doubt about marrying into this family," she said, her eyes brimming, "I no longer have such thoughts."

Robin felt he had gained a daughter, which was further assured when she asked him to drive her not only to the beauty parlor for her wedding-day hairdo but then on to the church for the ceremony itself. We were off to such a good start, but eventually there were the inevitable faux pas.

One unfortunate incident occurred when the then-newlyweds came home for a long weekend and went out with some of Andy's old pals. In typical maternal fashion, I was aghast when they didn't return until dawn, especially since our son was quite hung over the next day. Before the boys were married I'd try to handle these situations with humor, to let them know that while they made their own choices, I still noticed and cared. And so at breakfast I quipped, "Some way to treat your new bride."

"You've no right to dress him down," Shelly shot back. "How can you know if I was part of the plan or not? As it turned out, I had a perfectly fine time." Clearly I was no longer free to make my opinions quite so known.

The damnable thing about married children is their enormous need to create boundaries around their space. It's a veritable minefield we're meant to walk through, unsure where the explosives might be buried. A psychiatrist friend cautioned me that the closer you've been to your children, the farther they must go to break away. "They can't become adults in the presence of their parents," he continued. "Besides, they want to be new, different, and better than us. Isn't that what we tried to do when we first married?"

"OK. OK. I hear you," I said, cutting him off as his sentiments were annoying me. "But what am I to do with the unending ache of love I have for them? I don't want them to be burdened by my need. After all, elders are supposed to have it all together and be the ones without needs. But they're not dead, after all, only married! Robin says it's all about loss — that if he'd had his druthers he would never have given his boys

114

away. As for me, I just want to be able to share some real feelings now and again."

During a recent phone conversation with Andy, I did just that after being asked if Robin and I had enjoyed our recent visit with them.

"Actually, we were rather disappointed," I answered honestly. "Dad and I discussed it all the way home. We're having a hard time figuring out how to fit into your new life."

"Wow," he said, "I knew something wasn't right, but I couldn't figure it out. What can we do?" he asks, sounding as though he'd welcome suggestions.

"Well, you could start by giving us a little more time. Certainly your running takes up most of your spare time. Although I enjoyed the morning you took me to your marathon, out to that magnificent park filled with cactus, meeting your runner friends, and talking all the way out and back, it was our only time together. Before we invest in another visit we need to get your schedules and come when you aren't in training."

"And what else?" he asks, probing for more, typical behavior for him as he actually relishes addressing problems once they've surfaced.

"Well, your father wants to play more than one round of golf with you. He's hoping for some of those father-son moments that make him feel special and necessary."

"Dad said that?" he asked, incredulously.

"Yep, and guess what? I'm craving our old

talks, too — the ones where we'd bring up an issue and then we'd hammer away at it. We weren't afraid to be loud and argumentative before you were married, so why do we have to be so polite now?"

"I guess I thought we should be able to handle our lives on our own."

"Well, I've heard Shell on the phone asking her parents for advice. It hurts when you rarely consult us. I have almost thirty more years of living stashed away in the recesses of my consciousness," I say. "Surely a few of my opinions might be worth listening to."

His silence on the other end made me momentarily anxious, afraid that I had gone too far. So I filled the void with more explanation.

"A mother can't stop cherishing her children just because they up and get married or move away. Part of my reason for being is to encourage you when you're down and cheer for you when you're up. Isn't that what families are for?"

"I guess so," he admitted.

"And by now, I hope that I've demonstrated that I'm not going to interfere with your marriage."

"I know that, Mom," he said, sounding soft and sad. "You've given me a lot to think about. I'm glad we've cleared the air. We'll have to continue this conversation the next time we're together."

I wonder if we will. I hung up realizing that in the end, this is our issue, not theirs. They are too busy finding their way in the world to think about our relationship with them. Surely they just want it to work, somehow. Since I've had to figure out how to get along with my children from the beginning, why would it be any different now?

These thoughts and that phone conversation happened over two months ago, and now, in this white, blustery world, we await their safe arrival and prepare for a snowed-in visit. As I put the ingredients together for spiced cider, then turn to last-minute wrapping, I sense that I've been here before, waiting for these particular children. Today seems strangely reminiscent of the first time Andy brought her home — only then she was merely a girlfriend.

It was fall, not winter, and they were driving from Philadelphia, not flying from Phoenix, but in both cases they were late. We had put off dinner, which was to be casual Mexican fare as I had heard that Shelly was a vegetarian and I wanted an informal meal. Something told me this was not going to be an ordinary visit. I even persuaded Robin to let them decide if we would eat at the kitchen table or on the floor in front of the fireplace. Of course, to his dismay, they chose the floor, not the most comfortable place for my tall husband. But Robin pretended to enjoy the picnic while our son talked nonstop and loudly, typical behavior when he is excited or nervous. The next day at breakfast, it was the same thing — chatting for hours while nibbling on an oven-baked crepe. "I had this very same thing before," Shelly announced. "A woman in Minnesota made it for me when I was on my very first cross-country bike trip."

"Your what?" I asked, dumbfounded, my interest nevertheless piqued by this information. Indeed, this pint-size young woman was more formidable than she appeared, and those first couple of meetings felt like double dates. We fell in love with her right along with our son. Trouble was, I couldn't project to what lengths her impact would have on him. We were soon to find out that freedom would be the hallmark of their existence — from a courtship that took them camping in Alaska as well as biking across the country several times. It was on one of those adventures that, much to my chagrin, Andy developed a passion for the Rockies, and has sought jobs in the west ever since.

Perhaps I'm being punished for whisking Robin off to Africa, far from his destructive family life. And my mother before me? Didn't she happily flee from Brooklyn to Buffalo, eager to escape my father's mother, who doted on her only child? "Reap what you sow," the Bible says; that pretty much tells the story.

Mercifully, I'm constantly reminded of Kahlil Gibran's sentiments: "Your children are not your children," he cautions. "They come through you, but not of you. Though they are with you, they belong not to you. You may give them your love, but not your thoughts, for they have their own thoughts."

Still, I've always been a nester at heart, wishing to have the entire extended family living within driving distance. That is why, when Shelly mentioned offhandedly, and in a sort of voice that has documents to support it, that she prefers to live away from the influences of family — that visiting for a time and then taking leave is her preference — I was devastated. I had never imagined that our sons would leave home and only frequent the Cape for a week or two in the summer. Surely bringing them up near the ocean had to have infused their veins with the love of the sea.

I did try to fight their growing attachment to the other side of the country after too many glasses of wine one hot summer's evening, but only felt the fool for trying. Much to her credit, Shelly tried to assuage my sadness in a note written on stationery hand-painted by her:

I know that it's difficult for you to have us so far away. I also know that your ultimate desire is for us to live our lives in an authentic way. Your gift to Andy and me is to encourage us to find our true place — you do this and I notice and appreciate it. Right now that means it is in a place that is far from Cape Cod.

I can't expect you to fully grasp our feelings. I can only attempt to articulate our happiness. Over time I know you will gain a deeper understanding. It's OK that you feel the way that you do — it's only natural, you're a loving mother. My only hope is that you can see that it is in no way a rejection of you, or even the "East" as an entity, but an embracing of where we are now and how it feels.

Although she had the courage to address my sadness, she was also defining my feelings, how she hoped I would feel, leaving me with the burden of figuring how to reach across the continent and create the intimacy I crave.

Once again, I evoke some solace by retrieving a scene from Joan Erikson's life in which she was bidding her son farewell, probably for the last time, as he was returning to his home in Oregon. We had driven him to the bus station in Hyannis, and I watched their long embrace, after which he boarded the bus . . . then the final wave through the smoky glass window. I was struck by her stoicism, her acceptance of the inevitability of change, and her words to me thereafter: "Love is a wonderful thing, but it hurts."

Just now my eye is drawn to the cover of a church bulletin hanging on the refrigerator door with its pen-and-ink drawing of Madonna and Child and the inscription LOVE IS BORN written across the bottom. That is, after all, the message of Christmas — to make room in our hearts for those far away and in our home, for those who brighten the door. It's time now to embrace the moment. The next attempt is all that matters. I certainly don't want to miss out on happiness.

Like a child standing at a penny-candy counter with a limited amount of change, I must choose carefully that which I want to taste this holiday.

"Hey, honey," I call to my husband, who has just poured us each a glass of port, "could you put on some jolly music?" As James Galway's "In Dulci Jubilo" reverberates throughout the cottage, I wonder aloud if we should be worried about the children. "By now, I imagine them buried in a snowdrift somewhere between Providence and here."

"You're always so dramatic," Robin says, giving me a wink. "They'll be here soon. My guess is around five-thirty."

"You think?" I ask, welcoming his optimism. "Are you excited?"

"You know me," he says, leaning against the kitchen counter and cutting himself a piece of Brie. "I greet all these get-togethers with caution, sweetie. The kids are always new when they walk through the door. I govern myself accordingly."

I peer out the window, which has been brushed by drifting snow, and see that at some unnoticed moment it has stopped falling. I find myself willing them along as dusk begins to descend and the winds, with their fierce blizzardly sound, begin to pick up. I grab a broom to sweep off the porch and then laugh at my absurdity. They'll need to leave their car at the end of the road and trudge through the drifts getting wet and sloppy long before they make it to the door.

Back inside, I light the candelabra over the kitchen table and the other candles placed throughout the cottage as a welcoming gesture. After tossing a few more logs into the wood-stove, I burrow my head into my husband's broad chest and make the most of this peaceful moment before chaos descends.

And then I hear them — a distant giggle, boots stomping on the wooden porch, and a banging on the door as our son's booming voice roars "ho-ho-ho." They look like a couple of school-kids with knapsacks on their backs — he carries a duffel bag; she holds two beautifully wrapped gifts — all merriment and mirth. "Merry Christmas," our son says, bounding in the door, a veritable Santa Claus. "Talk about over the river and through the woods!" He drops his bags and comes toward me, arms outstretched, to plant a sloppy kiss on my cheek, the snow from his parka dampening my sweater, while Robin envelops our tiny daughter-in-law.

"Sure is a change from Arizona," Andy exclaims. "No doubt about it, we're having a white Christmas. I can't believe we're finally here. We probably could have driven in the same amount of time." He moves about the kitchen, lifting covers off pots, checking for goodies in the refrigerator, and grabbing a beer. Their excitement is catching.

"Here, let me take your cape, Shelly," Robin insists. "You must be wet and freezing."

"I'll be fine as soon as my fingers thaw out,"

she says, making a beeline for the woodstove, where she hovers for the next few moments. Her eyes dance in an impish way as she watches her husband's delight at home and holiday. "Look, Shell," he says, whipping an ornament that he made in first grade off the tree. "See what an artist I was, even back then."

We all laugh as he holds up a papier-mâché ball painted red and black, gaudily finished with sequins and gold glitter. I don't detect any guardedness in their movements or words, and I wonder if Andy's and my little phone conversation had some effect.

"Wow, this place feels so different in the winter," Andy exclaims as he draws a snowman on the steamy windowpane with his finger. "I love the tree in the kitchen," he exclaims. "Whose idea was that?" Without waiting for an answer, he checks the tags on some of the larger gifts, obviously curious to see if any are for him. "We're still into the tradition of exchanging a few gifts on Christmas Eve, right?" he asks, sounding as anxious as an eight-year-old.

"Whatever you say," I answer, wanting this night to be whatever they want. He seems jollier than usual, with no apparent desire to sit down. "Shell, would you like ginger ale or some hot cider?" he inquires of his wife, rushing across the room and giving her an unsuspecting peck on the cheek. I'm charmed.

"What's the plan for tonight?" he asks, always eager to know the agenda. "Surely we're not doing church in this weather."

"Are you kidding? I wouldn't be surprised if the service was canceled," I say. "There's stuff left to do for dinner. I'll need Shelly's help making the fondue," I continue, my first indication that we are including her family's culinary tradition in our Christmas. Tears fill her eyes and I see her vulnerability, a quality rarely shown by this seemingly together young woman. I want to embrace her, to make up for the fact that her parents are so far away. Sharing holidays is never easy, not when part of the myth insists that you go home for Christmas. But now these kids have two homes.

"C'mon, Shelly, help me get started with your recipe," I say, hoping that action will quell her momentary homesickness. She swallows her tears, dons an apron, and searches for the grater. "This is the easy part," she tells me. "Once it heats up, it's all in the stirring." I'm glad I thought to include her family's custom, as she is as proud of her roots as our son is of his. I remember overhearing a gentle argument between them over which family had the deeper Christmas rituals, and I was always charmed by her fondue story. "If you lose your bread in the pot while twirling it around on your fork, you must kiss your mate," she would tell me with glee.

As we grate the Gruyère, Emmentaler, and Swiss cheeses, then chop up the garlic, measure out the kirsch, and cut the French bread into cubes, I listen to her chatter and find myself thinking that the Chinese character for conflict — two women under the same roof — is all wrong. Sharing cooking tips and recipes, woman to woman, is a means by which one soul can open up to another. Welcoming her ideas instead of disregarding them opens up my perspective while closing the gap between us a little bit at a time. Show me a daughter-in-law who wants to follow in the footsteps of her mother-in-law, and I'll show you a saint! It feels good that my thoughts are loosening up. If I had chosen her or she me, everything would be different. But forcing two women together is an immediate detriment to good relations. No one wants to be told they must embrace another. Rather, it's more pleasant to discover another naturally.

I'm glad I like her just now. Since I was never blessed with a daughter, I've no choice but to cultivate any of the young women who stray into my life and welcome their modern ideas. Perhaps if she doesn't sense that I want anything more from her than friendship, we will eventually relax into an easy relationship.

Eventually the men beckon us into the living room and put cups of hot toddy in everyone's hand. I sink into a pillow in front of my husband's chair and lean back against his legs as our son moves to the couch where his wife is nestled among pillows, looking dreamy and tired. The service of Lessons and Carols from King's College, Cambridge, is on the stereo, providing just the right amount of church for us, and with plenty of smoked salmon and caviar canapés gracing the coffee table, we are about ready to settle in for a long winter's nap. As I melt into the moment, there appears to be ample room just now for input from both the young and the seasoned.

As a complicated version of "In the Bleak Midwinter" permeates the room our son drops his news.

"We won't be coming home this summer," he announces, his throat dry as he chokes on his words.

"What?" I ask in a high-pitched but casual tone, trying hard not to sound like I care.

"Well, we've made other plans," he continues, smiling now at his wife and being coy. My mind races. Are they planning another one of their far-flung trips or going to work in her parents' summer camp? Memorial Day weekend on the Cape has always been sacred. I can't believe that he's making such an announcement so soon after arriving home. I glance at my husband's poker face and then stare back into the flickering candles that are lighting up the coffee table.

"What we want to tell you is that around the end of July, you two are going to become grandparents."

"What?" I exclaim, feeling utter shock, attempting to process his words. "You're kidding," I blurt.

"We thought you'd be thrilled," he responds, puzzled now, his face registering disappointment.

"A baby?" I stutter, the word reverberating through my being. They hadn't given the slightest hint that starting a family was part of their immediate plan. I glance at my husband and see tears staining his cheeks, then glance back at the children's faces, which display the same. The reality of Andrew's words overtakes me as I experience the sanctity of the moment. Suddenly my past lies dormant. I find myself belonging only to the present.

"So this accounts for all your solicitous behavior around Shelly," I say, breaking up the sentimentality with some humor. "I thought it a little out of character that you were carrying her bags, offering her ginger ale instead of wine, and tucking pillows into the small of her back."

"You've trained him well, Joan," Shelly says, beaming as I flash back to my pregnancies and Robin doing the same. I'm made to celebrate the soft side of our sons — how both of them have been able to break through the harshness of masculinity.

"I think this calls for some champagne," my husband says, jumping up from his easy chair and racing off to the refrigerator. "We've had a bottle in there since the fall, just waiting for such a moment."

I run for the flutes, but not before giant hugs all around. As the cork pops, and he pours a round, I see the future bubbling up, like the endless fizz in each of our glasses. "To the unimaginable forever," I say.

"To the baby," my husband adds, "and if it happens to be a girl, something we haven't had in my family for generations, all of her needs will be taken care of."

Everything has shifted with the advent of a child. Robin and I step into a new realm, but a familiar one at least. In some ways we are being given a second chance, to improve on what we didn't do with our own family. In the words of William James, "I lie down in the stream of life and let it flow over me." I am reminded that life is not linear but circular, as I'd hoped it would be.

There is a gift tucked under the tree that begs to be opened right now. I retrieve it and hand it to my husband, who tears open the wrapping and begins to read the calligraphy inside the frame:

> *Our family is a circle of strength and love.*
> *With every birth and every union the circle*
>   *grows.*
> *Every joy shared adds more love.*
> *Every crisis faced together, makes the circle*
>   *stronger.*

"Obviously you bought this for me, but I think this is more appropriately hung in your house now," Robin says, handing it over to Andy, his large reservoir of feelings weighing down the room just now.

We are moving together naturally, linked now

by heritage, hers and ours. The walls that existed between us begin to crumble now. As the generations multiply, our existence as a unit somehow gets emphasized. There are volumes to be written — the still-unstoried parts of our lives. I see myriad chinks of light.

7

Riding the Storm

LATE JANUARY

If we have lived behind a mask all our lives sooner or later — if we are lucky — that mask will be smashed. Then we will have to look in the mirror at our own reality.

— Marion Woodman, *The Pregnant Virgin*

I have been rendered utterly and hopelessly vulnerable. It happened quite unexpectedly, as most accidents do. Robin and I had just left a local theater after a performance of *Our Town*. I was still wiping away tears and turning over Emily's soliloquy about life being too short and nobody really noticing the days while they're living them, when my feet hit a patch of black ice and splat, down I went.

"Are you all right?" my husband asked, extending his hand to pull me back up.

"Hardly," I answered feebly. "I can't move." I had no feeling whatsoever in my left foot, which dangled precariously from a rubbery ankle. As I sank into shock, frozen in place, and lay staring up at the sky, several strangers gathered around to help. Ten minutes later an ambulance was backing toward me, its ominous lights disrupting the darkness. Two medics hopped out, took one look at my deformed ankle, and lifted me onto a stretcher. Robin squeezed my shoulder and said he'd see me at the hospital. With sirens blaring and the vehicle moving at record speed, I lay chattering to the attendant as if I were at a cocktail party, attempting to push away the reality of the moment, not yet ready or willing to give in to my fate.

Ever since observing a friend who sprained her ankle a few days before Christmas, I had harbored thoughts about breaking some bone or another. When I went to visit her, there she sat in a rocking chair beside a blazing hearth, looking like the Madonna as her family scurried about doing the seasonal chores. I envied her situation — being waited on hand and foot at the busiest time of the year. But, just now, that picture didn't seem so appealing.

Once I was inside the emergency room, the drama began to unfold, as various nurses and technicians drew blood, tagged my wrist, took my vitals, and X-rayed my lungs, all the while smiling sweetly with a ubiquitous "poor dear" expression. Eventually there was a diagnosis: "A bi-malleolar fracture," the radiologist declared in an officious manner.

"Sounds grim to me," I uttered.

"Surgery is surely the next step," one of the nurses told me on the sly. "You'll be here until Thursday, at least."

I popped the Percocet offered to dull the pain, signed the consent forms, and decided on general anesthetic over a spinal. Twelve hours later I awoke, battered, bruised, and with a Demerol-induced headache. My husband was standing by looking more distraught than I. The doctor had just informed him that my recuperation would take a good eight weeks. So far, the "in sickness and in health" part of our marriage vows had meant to both of us only short spans of servitude not to exceed forty-eight-hour increments.

That was ten days ago. The entire experience continues to be a lesson in discomfort, both psychological and physical, as I go through various stages of withdrawal and anger, very much like the stages leading to death that Elisabeth Kübler-Ross describes. I'm adjusting to confinement, but not without a struggle. Waiting does not become me, nor does being out of control. How I wish I were a bit more adaptable, like Joan Erikson. When she was diagnosed with macular degeneration and had to contemplate encroaching blindness, she viewed the predicament as an opportunity to use her other senses. "I'll gather other sightless folk around me," she said, picturing the possibilities with relish, "and we'll sniff each other out. If that doesn't get us acquainted, we'll go to the next stage — licking!"

Unlike Joan, I'm without a plan as to how to cope with my incapacity, and I'm left to sit in our dreary bedroom with my leg propped up as if I'm in training for the fine art of laziness. I'm vacillating between giving in to my limitations or trying to overcome them. Unfortunately, upping the leg exercises and moving about briskly with the aid of crutches do little more than exacerbate the pain and exhaust me. So I'm left to receive, accept, and feel grateful for the lukewarm chicken noodle soup, oversteeped tea, and burnt toast that Robin brings me at mealtimes. To let myself be carried, to yield to unseen currents and be made to drift, is my primary challenge.

From my collapsed little world, I'm learning the true meaning of surrender — I am being forced to accept the fact that I've been stopped, and perhaps more discomforting, that things will no longer be done my way. Everywhere I look I see cracks in the system. On a recent trip to the bathroom, I noticed that not only was the toilet growing mold, but the door to the linen closet couldn't be shut because the sheets and towels were piled up so precariously. I am constantly regaled with the sound of his frustration: I listen to his swearing all the way down in the kitchen and the banging of pots and pans as he stores them away in a manner that sounds to me like he's feeling put upon. Yesterday I sniffed smoke as it crept from the kitchen, through the living quarters, and up the stairs toward the bedroom, where it set off the alarm. As Robin stomped up the stairs to turn the damn thing off, making noises meant to elicit sympathy every step of the way, I sank under the covers in an effort to keep my mouth shut.

"I left the oatmeal on the stove while loading the car for the dump," he explained, without being asked. "This housekeeping stuff is tricky . . . it's all in the timing, right?" I could do nothing but nod in agreement. Before this, I would have jumped into action at the first sound of his distress because I didn't want to experience his aggravation. But just now I can't, and I'm finding the best way to handle my expectations or desires is not to have any.

I'm trying to tuck away my criticisms and excuse his domestic ineptitudes. After all, he's had no training. We've never divvied up the household chores before this, and I've certainly never bothered to share my litany of obsessive household practices.

Take the laundry, for instance. According to me, to do the job right you must separate the dark colors from the light, be sure not to overload the machine, and fold the towels in threes so that they will fit neatly on the shelf. I have a similar set of steps for washing dishes — you let the silver and glassware soak in the dishpan first since those are the utensils that touch your lips. Then you tackle the plates and finally the pots.

But I've learned that making suggestions will do little more than incur his wrath. No matter how I phrase them, my comments will come out sounding like cranky criticism. "Trust this time with quiet and respect," so says Taoist wisdom, "and listen for the messages." I try to ask myself, Do I really care how he does the laundry or about the manner in which he cleans the dishes so long as the jobs get done? Besides, *beggars can't be choosers.*

Still, because he is the kind of man who likes to succeed at whatever he does, I fear that his positive attitude might turn negative as my convalescence drags on. Robin has never had to sustain caretaking before. There were small moments: bringing the babies to me for their middle-of-the-night nursings; massaging me with ointments and applying hot compresses when my back went out; standing by me at the doctor's office when we found out that the lump in my breast was not a tumor but a spider bite; and the romantic one, when he washed my hair over the kitchen sink, after I'd sprained a finger. Although we didn't end up making mad, passionate love as had Robert Redford and Meryl Streep when he washed her hair in *Out of Africa*, remembering that moment helps me to realize that being helpless or weak has its place in the life of a marriage — that to let down one's guard, to be touched for reasons other than sex, can carry a couple to an unexpected level of intimacy.

Besides, isn't it about time that I collect on a job done well over the past thirty years? Although it never occurred to me to invoice my husband and kids for such things as dinners cooked (11,000), parties planned (700 at least), errands run (inestimable), favors and emergencies at a rate of, say, five a day (55,000), perhaps I've accrued more than my share of sick leave. Role reversal, although uncomfortable at first, is probably just what we need right now, especially since it is obvious that the previous balance of power was upended long ago.

If I dare to tell the truth, I can't point the finger at Robin for that dynamic. Perhaps I wanted to be a helpless female, but subconsciously I sought a mate who would let me wear the pants, because I never really trusted anyone. I suppose my mother passed on her own control issues to me. No one could do anything as well as she could, which just about left my father out of the finances, entertaining, travel plans, and raising of the children. What's more, she was always advising me to contribute and give. What I didn't realize was that givers retain the control while receivers are left to be vulnerable and gracious. I've never found it comfortable to receive — not gifts, compliments, sex, or even attention. It's astonishing how quickly we fall into a cycle of withholding. Somewhere along the way, I began to believe that the real problem was not my ability to receive, but his inability to give what I needed. The lack of trust intensified the problem and forced me to hold myself apart from Robin. I was the only person capable of taking care of my happiness, my fun, my very life! But without give-and-take, how can love survive?

I'm suddenly filled with remorse over the damage I've done. Robin has left for the dump and the market, so I've no one with whom to share these thoughts. Instead, I begin to sort and tidy the dresser drawers he left on the bed, an activity I resorted to as a child when I was sick for any length of time. Any task, however small, gives credence to my day. After tossing out frayed stockings, worn T-shirts, and some ancient costume jewelry, I find a stack of greeting cards and notes tucked safely beneath my underwear. There's a valentine from my husband, several notes from my sons, a letter from my dear father, the eulogy I wrote for his funeral, and more. My tired mind spins uneasily. As images long imprisoned come to the surface, I find myself in a puddle of tears.

Separation comes up again and again in these letters. The first note I unfold is a crumpled piece of notebook paper on which Andy had scribbled a birthday greeting back in 1985, just before he left for college.

Dear Mom,

You're a thinker and so am I. Often our thinking leads us to fantastic ideas and delightful feelings. But sometimes our thinking makes us think that for some reason we screwed up and we're failing. When those times come we should calm down, relax, and remember all the good things we do and are capable of doing. Because those things far outnumber our screw ups.

We've spent a good part of this year disagreeing but I think those disagreements have brought us closer together as friends. It's easy for me to talk to you and I know that if I screw up I'll be able to come to you and you'll put me into shape. I hope that now that you're 42 you can have faith to come to me when you think you've screwed up so that I can straighten you out like you do to me.

This is the last birthday of yours that I'll be home for probably some time and I hope you enjoy it. You and Dad have spoken about how you'll miss me next year but I'm going to miss you guys just as much. Remember, I couldn't have made it this far without you so keep it up and maybe I'll turn out O.K.

With Love, Andy

I smile at his youthful confidence as well as the depth of our connection. He really intended to be there for me. Obviously as anxious about leaving as I was about having him go, my son was assuring me that I was his friend, not just his mother. He didn't realize that life was about to get in the way and separate us. His sentiments are both sweet and sad — but sentiments, none-theless, that I shall always cherish.

And then, months later, seasoned by college, his ego strengthening as he discovers the world, he had newfound wisdom to offer.

Dear Mom,

Well, here I am. I bet you thought you'd go through the entire year without getting a letter from me. But since it's Mother's Day I wanted to write — not get you a card, that's phony. I'd rather show you my feelings on paper.

When I left home for school last September I knew it would be difficult for you to adjust without seeing me every day. But I think you've adjusted well. Before I graduated from high school you were always there for help and hindrance. I know that I'm starting to grow up a little but I sincerely hope that we can maintain our long precious friendship forever.

I know you think of me quite a bit because I think of you a lot as well. On this Mother's Day I would just like to convey a few words of wisdom. First, don't overwork yourself. You're a competitor and a winner. You needn't constantly strive further. Find a comfortable style and stick with it. Don't grow old but be consistent. It'll be much better for everyone. Second, take it easy with Luke. He is a great kid, he just steps to the beat of a different drummer and I admire that. You should too. Third, make sure you allow Dad to help you. Don't always force yourself on him. Let things come. Remember, love means never having to say sorry. That's an immortal ideal.

Well, that's my sermon but I thought as it's Mother's Day and all I might as well attempt a few words of inspiration to you, my best friend.

I love you Ma . . .

P.S.
May God bless and keep you always, May your wishes all come true.
May you always do for others and let others do for you.

*May you build a ladder to the stars and climb on
every rung
And may you stay . . . forever young. Dylan*

I can hear the tune as if it is blaring from his
stereo in a nearby room and feel blessed by his
wishes for me: to be consistent, to not overwork,
to let Robin help. If only he could see his dad
now! Still, I feel sad that he picked up on our
marital discontent back then. It's funny how we
deceive ourselves into thinking that we actually
fool children with our ambiguity. The psycho-
therapist Carl Jung felt it was the responsibility
of parents to do everything in their power not to
lead a life that could harm the children. And perhaps more dauntingly he suggested that "what
usually has the strongest psychic effect on the
child is the life which the parents have not
lived."

Strong words to digest, with the concerns in
Andy's letter in mind. Because he loved and
cared for me, I sense he wanted me to begin to
taste something of adventure as he was about to
do. Out of the mouths of babes . . .

Next there's a journal entry, written on my
way home from Chicago after a visit with my
younger son, Luke, and his then-girlfriend
Susannah.

*I said farewell to my son today. It had been a
while since I had come to visit him. There he
was, proud as punch in his humble little apart-*

ment, happily ensconced with his girlfriend of one and a half years. I walked right in on a newly formed grown up and when I said good-bye at the airport, I realized my tears were not so much about until we meet again, rather they were about good-bye to my boy, good-bye to who he was when I was his protector — good-bye to before.

I look at my handsome young strapping son and I know there will be another time — many more other times — but still, he will never quite be as he was on this visit. I know that because he has changed so since last we met. So why am I crying? He's growing up — don't I want that? Of course I do. It's just that the relationship will never have the ease it once had when we came in and out of each other's lives so regularly that I could notice the little nuances about him and he about me.

At the gate as I walked through the security and turned to look, he was there — waving his little boy gentle wave — and then I walked around the corner and he appeared again at another window. Did he not want to see me go? Does he still need me? Is he sad after all, or relieved? Now the tears started to come but I smiled hard in an effort to keep them in my eyes, my chubby cheeks acting like a dam, and then he motioned me on.

Reading these sentiments, written in the moment, offers raw evidence that is further helping to resolve my grief around the boys' growing up and leaving. I sense now that I need to let that which is broken mend: not only the ankle but the invisible power struggle in my relationships and with my family. It is no coincidence that the left side of my body sustained the injury, as it is the left side that is thought to be the feminine side — the side that receives and surrenders. In the healing of my ankle, am I also meant to allow my softer energies to flow more freely?

I turn to more memorabilia waiting for me under a silky nightgown — a lacy valentine that Robin bought in a gift shop, not off a drugstore rack. There is no formal message, leaving plenty of room for a personal inscription. "To my one and only Valentine . . ." he writes. "You are entitled to as many kisses as you wish, today and forever."

"Really," I recall asking him while puckering up and waiting for the first installment. "This could be fun," I said, my eyes flashing in a naughty way, as I demanded kiss number two just moments later. I lean my head back on the pillow and wonder if such moments are to be in my future.

The call to understand myself involves remembering. Reading these mementos today not only defines who I am becoming but reminds me of how inextricably intertwined I am with my children, even though we are not in and out of each other's daily lives. They affirm family, heritage, and provide the very rationale for my marriage. I sit here not with a mirage or a pile of delusions but with hard evidence that swells my pride and passion.

My broken ankle has turned out to be a blessing. Last year I had legs for mobility and plenty of opportunity to run off and seek. Now, doomed to slowness, I've been bestowed with idle time that forces me inward. This brief interlude with my past is reaping benefits for my future.

I must have dozed off, as I didn't hear Robin returning from the grocery store or approaching the bedroom. I come out of my dreamy state to see him standing beside the bed, holding a long-stemmed pink rose and seeming eager, as if he's dying to bring me news from the outside world.

"Welcome back!" I whisper, my brief yawn turning into a soft smile. "What's up?"

"Nothing really, except how good you look."

"You'll make me blush," I answer.

"What's that?" he asks, pointing to the valentine.

"Don't you remember — the year of the kisses and what that led to?"

He nods in an embarrassed sort of way, perhaps because lovemaking has not been on our list of priorities. I reach for him in order to enjoy a big hug.

He pulls away, anxious, it seems, for something else.

"We're lunching in the kitchen today," he says. "C'mon, roll those legs over the side of the bed and I'll help you up." I'm not sure what this is all about, since I have been taking all my meals in bed, but I'm not about to argue. With crutches under my arms, I hobble toward the landing, sit on the top step, send the crutches sliding to the bottom, and then slip myself down step by step. Once on the main floor, I am invigorated to be back in the heart of this place. What's more, it feels inviting and looks remarkably neat. As I navigate through the living room, and then the dining area, I'm increasingly curious as to what I'll find in the kitchen.

Surprise! The place is immaculate — counters devoid of clutter, the stove top glistening, shiny plates stacked neatly in the dish drainer, and fresh flowers on the table, which is set with good china and wine goblets. I silently chastise myself for thinking that he couldn't possibly keep the house together. "Gosh, everything looks so organized. Whatever have you done?" I exclaim.

Like a housewife who is eager to justify a mundane day, he's quick to point out a pot rack he's hung over the island and the newly purchased microwave he tells me he couldn't have lived without when he was living alone. "I took most of the junk that was cluttering the countertops to the thrift shop," he says. "Wait until you see inside the cupboards and drawers. They're right back to the way you originally had them. I know, I know, you were right. I was being obstinate and ridiculous when I rearranged everything last fall."

We've been touched by an accident, I think as he babbles on — his attitude ebullient. How I've been waiting all these years to be roused and rescued. Has he finally become the man I described to my parents when I wrote to them from Africa?

He motions for me to take my seat on the bench near the pine table and quickly brings a footstool on which I can prop my leg. I await the feast, which begins with a cup of mushroom bisque and continues on to Caesar salad topped with shrimp, all of this accompanied by a cool sauvignon blanc. I shake my head at this man, raised in a doctor's household with a live-in housekeeper, who was sent away to boarding school and knew nothing of servitude, rising now to the occasion. We seem to be taking our voyage away from the safety of the shore, no longer tied to the familiar roles of the past. Some sort of spiritual regeneration is occurring, and I'm basking in the moment.

"I'd finally like to have that conversation we started after the theater around Emily's speech," I say, taking a sip of my wine.

"You mean when she asks the Stage Manager if human beings ever realize life while they live it?" he asks.

"That's it. We should be made to read her soliloquy often," I say, "until we finally realize that it's only the present moment that matters."

He begins reciting the lines from memory, having done the play in summer stock. " 'Good-by, Good-by, world. Good-by, Grover's Corners, Mama and Papa. Good-by to clocks ticking . . . and Mama's sunflowers. And food and coffee. And new-ironed dresses and hot baths . . . and sleeping and waking up. Oh, earth, you're too wonderful for anybody to realize you.' "

We sit, eyes glazed, quietly content.

"You know, lying in bed all day, I've been forced, like Emily, to notice the tiniest things: a spider building a web in the corner of our bedroom and how strangely the cat purrs when she's in a deep sleep. I've certainly noticed the upgrade in my meals . . . from burnt toast to omelettes, no less, and Campbell's chicken noodle to mushroom bisque. And, whatever made you start frequenting the health food store?"

He seems almost as pleased with himself as I am with him. The small values that Thornton Wilder illustrated in *Our Town* are emerging as the ones I care about most.

"I never could bear to really listen to Emily deliver that speech," he says. "There was rarely a dry eye in the audience, I guess because few of us concern ourselves with the preciousness of life. Before you're really launched, it seems, you're saying good-bye. Too many good-byes." His voice drifts off and then he clears his throat. "The time is past for good-byes. I'm more interested in hello."

It feels as if we're in a play, not talking over the table about real life. It's been said that love's deep realization is found in the growing, struggling, longing, and reaching toward perfection, all the while living fully in the here and now. My inability to receive love has been broken down by my need to accept care. In a weakened position I have no choice but to feel, notice, and respond. "What is destructive is impatience, haste and expecting too much, too fast," said May Sarton. The principles of humility and openness will keep me going.

8

Dropping Anchor

LATE MARCH

A man travels the world over in search
of what he needs and returns home to find it.

— George Moore, *The Brook Kerith*

I'm out and about now, occasionally hobbling on crutches or with the help of my "moon-boot," a gray plastic on-again-off-again brace that supports the bones, which are not yet healed. Still, I'm far from mobile. With two stick-shift cars between us and my foot too weak to manage the clutch, I'm left to be chauffeured by Robin when I crave a different landscape. For the most part, I stay holed up in the bedroom, where we've spent the past few weeks talking about our future.

What has emerged is an apparent desire on both our parts to pack up the tent and set down some permanent stakes. It's been said that when a friendship is in trouble you need to change the rhythm of how and when you see each other. Role reversal has changed our pattern, and, most particularly, new ideas are surfacing with Robin.

"Y'know, I'm coming to the conclusion that the Cape is a good place," he announced after returning from a morning of errands, as if recognizing it for the first time. "Right now, I honestly can't imagine living anywhere else."

"Really," I countered. "What makes you so sure?"

"I'm beginning to feel that maybe I *can* make a difference here."

"How so?" I asked, wondering what had transpired in the short span of a morning.

"Well, I ran into one of the selectmen downtown. He asked if I would consider running for school committee. I can't figure out how he even knew I'd had anything to do with education, but the idea intrigues me."

"Well, that's a small town for you," I answered. "I'm surprised about the fact that he approached a nonnative, though. It's pretty unusual for New Englanders to reach out to someone who wasn't born here."

He offered me a satisfied smile. "What do you think? Should I go for it? I'd have to man a campaign, you know." His voice was already imbued with more than the normal complement of enthusiasm.

"Can't see why not. You've been looking for meaningful work and now here it is, plopped in your lap. Kind of neat being drafted instead of going after it on your own, isn't it?"

He shook his head in an astonished sort of way. "It all began at the barbershop," he said. "Several customers got into a heated discussion about the capping of the landfill. I didn't know there could be so many opinions. One guy wants it to become a nine-hole golf course. Someone else is afraid our taxes will be raised because carting the garbage off Cape will cost a fortune. Another was talking about the environment. It was wild! I'm getting an inkling of why my father would stop in to see Tiny the florist every day before work and then head over to Sal's newspaper stand to discuss town politics. Looking back, that was his entertainment, his way to stay connected to something outside of his job."

As I listen and indulge in his good energy, I'm struck that all this is happening to my husband during the worst month of the year. Most Cape Cod natives bolt if they can during March, no longer able to tolerate the damp, gray days. I figure if you can manage to like a place when it's at its bleakest, chances are you'll like it forever.

"So, is this about to be one of those epiphany moments?" I finally ventured to ask.

"Could be," he answered with a twinkle.

It's marvelous how forces of blind life work their magic when we least expect it. Even though we married and went far away, there was always this place waiting for us. The land was a wedding gift from Robin's parents, a grand gesture on their part — his father's money being invested for us near my parents' cottage. They must have foreseen that such a gift would mean we'd be spending less time near them on the Jersey shore. Yet they knew the value and importance of owning land. Robin's grandfather had a large farm that he eventually sold off, and he used the money to found a bank and retire early.

Our tiny plot will never be worth a great deal, but it has served grand purposes nonetheless. As the poet Wendell Berry says, "No place is a place unless something happened there . . . a place you come back to time and again and stay long enough to learn from it . . . a place that eventually forces nostalgia on you."

The Cape is where we came upon returning from Africa. It's where our first child was born and both sons were baptized, where they learned to walk, ride tricycles, swim, and eventually sail. It is where they brought their girlfriends, worked at summer jobs, grew to know their maternal grandparents intimately, and were blessed in a tiny, seafaring church before they embarked on marriage. But most significantly, throughout our marriage, it has served as a bridge between Robin and me when the rivers of disappointment overflowed. Each time we returned, even if it was only for the weekend, there stood the cottage — a welcoming mother with her arms outstretched. After uncovering the wicker and rolling up the blinds, it took only minutes for us to feel a sense of home. No matter our mood on the ride up, an emotional truce was always ours for the taking as contentment took over and we melded back into one again. Could it be that now it is supporting our very reconciliation?

"So, what are you saying?" I probed, and then held my breath in anticipation.

"I guess I'm seeing that this is one of the few remaining real towns on the planet. Hell, there's a golf course five minutes away, a sweet church in the center of town, simple people, a rural environment, and the best beaches in the world. What more could I ask for?"

Confluence is a magical thing. How he came to own his new attitude, I wouldn't venture to guess, but as I listened to the lilt in his voice I felt that we were coming together; a convergence was occurring, two separate forces now combining, no longer resisting, but aligning.

That seminal moment was several weeks ago. Since then we've started to think once again and with more earnest intent about enlarging the cottage. Ideas have been spewing forth, mostly out of Robin's mouth, as we begin the renovation of our lives. "We'll need to raise the roof," he says. "That will give us two proper rooms instead of just the loft, where the ceiling is barely high enough for me to stand, anyway."

I feel a tinge of melancholia because the loft has kept our lifestyle camplike and casual. Maybe I'm just chafing at the word *proper,* which connotes fancily made beds, knickknacks, dust ruffles with matching poufs, and more frills.

"Personally, I think we should push out toward the woods," he continues, "and create a country kitchen. With one baby on the way and more to come, God willing, we'll need extra dining space, don't you think? I see a long pine table where the children can play board games, paint pictures, and such . . . all the stuff you used to do with the boys when they were little."

His exuberance is catching. But isn't he getting a little too grand — and where are we getting the money? "You know, dear," I say, "after emptying out one house and winnowing most of our possessions, I can't see expanding too much. I'm more prone to editing."

"Well, for once I want a den — a place of retreat where I can do as I please," he announces, a throb of conviction and passion in his voice. "Up until now my private space has amounted to an easy chair in the living room. You're always talking about sacred space. Well, I'll be damned if I don't get some for myself this time!"

He has never really bonded with any of our houses, and I had always longed for him to have this kind of enthusiasm. I quickly abandon my objections, holding back my picky questions, and decide to play with my ideas on paper. Fortunately, he hardly notices and continues with his bursts of brainstorming. I'm reminded of an Amish saying — "Men make houses. Women make homes" — as he speaks of gutting, expanding, and cantilevering. It's amusing to see very specific ideas busting out of a man who finds little enjoyment in household chores and fixes things only when they break. A sweet earnestness is overshadowing his normal brooding personality. I'm feeling a peace that only comes from yielding.

Nonetheless, we need a conduit just now to keep the peace alive as we embark on the difficult task of reimagining our home. I've chosen my dear friend Cheryl, a wonderful designer, to help Robin and me blend our thoughts and create a mutually desirable reality. Our friendship began twelve years ago, and together we have weathered each other's personal storms. Cheryl's gift on a job is to absorb the energy not only of the place but of the people who inhabit it. She believes that a house holds your dreams. "You put up new walls with nothing more than sticks and mortar, but once inside, the energy bubbles up from those who inhabit the space," she told me once. As a result, she prefers to actually move into the house while she's reconfiguring the space until her ideas for the transformation are utterly clear.

Luckily when I called to ask her if she would come, she was coincidentally between jobs and anxious to take a break from her immediate life. She's been here for three days now, her drafting table set up in the middle of the living room, next to the French doors, which offer her optimum light as well as a view of the very space where she is proposing our addition. Days flow like fine wine. Robin exits early for a round of golf, I retire to my office to keep my writing career blossoming (my earning power now more important than ever), and dear Cheryl, her third cup of coffee in hand, sits engulfed with pencil, paper, templates, and electric erasers as she draws and sketches, her hands moving to the rhythm of Celtic music playing gently in the background.

Over lunches of soup, salad, or leftovers from the previous night, she holds court like a marriage counselor, her accommodating mind careful to include each of our visions as she skillfully ushers us into the unknown. "You must search within yourselves to figure out what your requirements are for a sense of well-being," she advises. This is a novel idea, since for most of our married life we've been of the belief that home is not much more than a place that feeds and sleeps family and friends. "No, no," she insists, always with a sideward glance to catch the nuances of our reactions. "Be a little mad . . . dream a bit. You don't have to act on your musings, but they'll add color and life to the project."

My mind wanders back to all of my childhood homes, where my mother would call in an artist and have the inscription "Home is where the heart is" painted on the kitchen wall. Now, in the middle of my adulthood, the sentiment feels essential for living the rest of my days. Other than that, I can't visualize how the cottage will be reconfigured, and I rarely know what I think until I see a rendering of what I say. Fortunately, Cheryl's drawings quickly give clarity and form to what I am unable to articulate. Each day we anticipate her vision of our ideas like art connoisseurs before an important unveiling.

"I want to bring all the seasons inside," I tell her. "When it was just a summer place it hardly mattered as we rarely came home before dark.

But now we'll be inside during winter and spring, and I can't be separated from the soothing Cape light. I need the sunrises and sunsets, the evening shadows and murky fog, the starry skies and harvest moons. Can I have it?"

Within twenty-four hours she produces a picture of a new wing with plenty of eastern exposure, skylights in strategic locations, and wraparound floor-to-ceiling windows on the side of the cottage that faces the forest.

"Well, aesthetics are all well and good," Robin pipes up while pacing about like a tiger in a cage, "but I want breathing space. As far as I'm concerned, we could push out in several directions and I'd still feel contained."

"How about raising the ceilings?" Cheryl suggests, deftly assuaging him. I breathe a sigh of relief when she talks height instead of square footage. "We could easily open things up in the living and dining rooms and the new kitchen as well. With all the tall men in your life, I couldn't agree more."

He seems content with her suggestion but quickly redirects the discussion to the topic of his den. I wouldn't mind if he didn't already have a room of his own, but there is already the office he created at considerable expense in the basement.

"What do you see as the function of your den?" Cheryl asks. She doesn't entertain any additions or corrections without a valid purpose.

"You know, just a place to kick back . . . a

man's room, with a leather chair, some book-shelves, and, of course, a television and stereo. In fact, I'd like to wire the entire house for sound."

"Television!" I exclaim. "The cottage has never had such an intrusion. Haven't we kept it that way because it is a refuge from outside inter-ference?"

"Well, yes," he agrees, "but that was before we came here permanently. We can't continue to cut ourselves off. Besides, when the boys come, part of the fun is watching sports together. You know that."

"You make a good point," Cheryl says, much to my chagrin, as she wanders about the living room. "You could close in the porch. It would mean moving your main entrance to the side, over there," she continues, pointing toward the back of the present kitchen. "But then we could create a nice little foyer that would connect the new kitchen to the rest of the house, and better yet, you wouldn't have to push out to create Robin's den."

"Yeah, but what about the television?"

"If he can close the door, what difference does it make?" Cheryl asks, sounding more like his friend than mine. "But I agree with you about the sound system. Being in the middle of the woods as you are, the sounds should be what we're hearing now . . . birds chattering, the rustle of leaves, and your wind chimes."

"OK, so I'm overruled on the television situation," I say, "but I'm also thinking about the baby that is on the way. Is there a quiet corner where we can create a small nursery? I hated visiting my parents when the boys were little, trying to settle them down for naps and bedtime with all the commotion going on in the rest of the house."

"Talk about designing a life!" Cheryl exclaims. "You're certainly looking down the road. I'll have to work that in when I get the entire floor plan figured out. I've got more than the essentials to work with."

I'm amazed at how this process is forcing us to imagine the pattern by which we intend to live. Until now we've been floating here, drifting there, both of us for one reason or another afraid to chart a unified course. She is willing us toward continuity, not only in the structure of the house but in the values we've come to hold, making us review and renew our vows — not the ones stated in the wedding ceremony, but the ones we've been establishing along the way.

"These plans are an exercise in hope," Cheryl says. "Hopefully we're creating familiar shelter that can hold experiences for your children and grandchildren."

"In that case, we'd best not interrupt the interior too much, as the memories are apt to evaporate," I answer, feeling now that I am the carrier of all culture, as Ashley Montagu called women.

"There's always the shell path," Cheryl assures me. "Didn't the boys collect those shells and bring them back from the beach when they were small? And we won't be touching the tree house or the door frame where you've measured everyone's height from year to year. We'll keep it stark and simple — a Shaker look might add style but not harm the integrity. And think monochromatic, use only natural paint tones and keep the color muted, austere, yet warm, like the sea on an overcast day. The children and what they bring home from the beach will be the bulk of your accessories."

From impulse to final design we are reshuffling space in order to create a perennial place. There is hope for any couple who earnestly constructs their own shelter — not unlike the commitment to have children. You believe enough in your combined strengths to go ahead, even though you are unsure how your mutual values will surface once the final product appears. No matter. This adventure is shaking us up and providing new energy to our lives. Like the recalcitrant forsythia that will soon announce springtime, our cozy cottage is about to burst its seams in the name of family.

This being Cheryl's last night here, we're having a girls' night out. We've bought ourselves a very good bottle of merlot and are heading off to a town landing where we can drive the car nearly down to the water's edge. After opening the windows in order to hear the slurping and sloshing of high tide as it creeps gradually up toward the car, we uncork the wine and dip crackers in

Boursin cheese. In the denouement she unveils her initial floor plans, spreading the whole of my new world over the dashboard. "It's a masterpiece!" I exclaim.

"I call it the ultimate collaboration," Cheryl answers, and then without preamble continues, "I can't believe how flexible and creative Robin has been. He's a changed man, my friend. You should feel very fortunate."

I am stunned. We have spent years complaining about our husbands behind their backs, so her comment is totally unexpected. "How so?" I ask.

"I was there when he wouldn't come to your rescue — all those years of gloomy moods, when he'd stand apart and never be fully involved. Relationship with Robin was tangential, at best. But no longer. Not only did he have some great ideas, but he was often sweetly deferential. Oh, he knew what he wanted for himself, that's for sure. And it was amusing watching him pace about the room spouting ideas like an executive giving dictation to his secretary, but he was also sensitive to your desires and considered what the family visits will require."

"Well, I have to admit that his spatial ideas were right on," I say. "But don't be fooled by his good nature. He could just as easily revert back to the old Robin when you leave. To tell you the truth, I think he enjoyed being fawned over by two women for a week. He'd make a good Mormon! The truth is, you're a damn good conciliator." I tip my glass. "Here's to you, friend, for your creative genius. Looking at these preliminary plans, I'm thrilled that the cottage will have so much flow."

"Well, it was Robin who insisted on the openness," she demurs.

I must admit to feeling a sense of relief, hearing her characterize my husband. After all, she is one of the few persons to view what's going on between us since he retired. Her affirmation somehow validates that Robin and I are actually headed in new directions.

The high tide has pushed up to the front tires, forcing us to back up. I turn on the ignition, back out of the boat launch, and take one last look at the expanse of cove. It appears that Robin and I have flung the anchor overboard. It is burrowing itself into the sea's sandy bottom. The past is a different country now. Our voyage seems to be leading us into a safe harbor.

9

All Hands on Deck

MAY

History is everywhere. It seeps into
the soil, the subsoil. Like rain,
or hail, or snow, or blood.

— Edna O'Brien,
House of Splendid Isolation

Our life is topsy-turvy. With the exception of our bed and dresser, a table, and a few chairs, we have hauled all the furniture to the cellar. Carpenters, plasterers, roofers, and masons have descended upon the cottage, eager to tear apart what it was, to create what it will become. There's something cathartic about breaking down one structure to build another — like children at the beach, gleefully smashing one sand castle in order to begin the next one.

But I wasn't prepared for the amount of demolition that has taken place in a matter of days. All of a sudden, a bulldozer and backhoe appeared and chopped away at our front yard, taking down some of my favorite oaks and the giant pine I had planned to cover with twinkling lights at Christmas. I'm certain that my newly planted tulip bulbs were churned up in the rubble as well.

I try to remind myself that endings and beginnings always go together, but such counsel offers little consolation to someone who has a difficult time with transitions. I'm one to cry at the stroke of midnight on New Year's Eve, sad to see the passing of another year. I avoid good-byes like the plague, especially when I know I won't be seeing the person for quite some time. The only hopeful spin I can put on the balding of our property is that it occurred on May Day, a day originally set aside to honor newly paired couples and sprouting crops. Perhaps there is a good omen brewing here.

Still, I knew that this domestic work in progress would wreak havoc with both my psyche and the new equilibrium of our relationship, especially since we are occupying the very space in which all the work is being done. My office has become our bedroom, and the contractor has promised to leave the stove, refrigerator, and counters in place until the new kitchen has been created. The bucolic days of yore are now confounded by the screech of power tools and the noise of workers dressed in their denim overalls and heavy boots, with hammers and tape measures hanging from their sagging belts, stomping around in the dirt and sawdust, rock music blaring from portable radios. But no matter. I'm of the opinion that in order to truly restore flow in a relationship you need myriad challenges.

It was a happy fantasy, working with Cheryl, interviewing contractors, putting together a budget. We approached this next phase as a bride and groom await their wedding day — buying into the fun, the drama, the pretty picture, without looking too closely at the hard realities.

"Do you think we're up to this?" I asked Robin.

"Sure," he answered, unusually upbeat. "Hard is good. There's no doubt that this project poses a challenge to my entire personality, which is predominantly lazy, but it's also an education."

I breathed a sigh of relief, feeling a little more confident. At least one of us believed that all the chaos was worth it. Actually, the only thing that has gone wrong so far is that the cat has disappeared. First, the bulldozer sent her up the very tree it was about to knock down, then, with the invasion of the dump truck, she ran off to the neighbors', and two days ago, when the carpenters invaded the interior and plugged in their electric saws, she took off for good, I fear.

It's funny, but for years I never wanted to settle here for good, at least not until I was certain that the magic wouldn't wear off. I never minded renting out the cottage and only using it before and after the summer season. We were quite content camping out with friends or my parents, when they rented a place.

The original cottage was built cheaply, and for years we patched it together as damage demanded. Those were the days when entertaining was simple: We invited people home straight from the beach, set out a plate of cheese and crackers, and gave them drinks. The cottage's interior was so sparse, with nothing much for anyone to steal, that we never bothered to even lock the door. Gradually, however, we upgraded until it became a comfortable summer refuge, and now we're determined to breathe more permanent life into it. At least that's what I think we're doing.

Our days begin at dawn. No more coffee and talk in bed. We're up, dressed in our tattered and paint-stained overalls and working before the coffee has even finished perking. Since we want to save money and participate directly in the process, we've assumed responsibility for a good deal of the prep work — lifting old linoleum, tearing out the worn industrial carpet, unhinging doors, ripping out the bathroom vanities and kitchen cabinets, and, best of all, taking a sledgehammer to the Sheetrock walls and watch them crumble down. Most mornings find us moving forward without words, feeling our way to the next chore until one of us shares a silly thought.

"You're hitting away at that wall as if you're really getting a kick out of this," I say to Robin as he all but destroys the Sheetrock that has previously divided the kitchen from the living room.

"Not as much fun as you seem to be having tossing the pieces overboard," he says, watching me fling window frames, walls, and wood trim out the window to a waiting Dumpster below. "I never imagined that this job would be a catharsis," he says between heaves. "Either that or I'm purging myself of more anger than I ever thought I had."

"Whatever," I answer. "We're getting the job done."

"It actually feels like theater to me," he says, his voice wandering off. "All those sets that I built and then struck."

"And the cast of characters, like these strangers working on our stage right now," I add. "I'll tell you one thought I've been playing with, though. It's fun to be working together."

"I agree," he confesses, "since I never thought I'd like working with you."

"Well, I hope that's changed!" I say, waiting for him to hand me a kinder remark.

"Actually it has, especially since I give most of the orders," he says with a wink.

"Damn you," I say, slapping him gently with my dusty work glove as we settle into a laugh. "You know, this culture has done a terrific job of separating husbands and wives after they marry. The man goes off to an office, the wife goes to another office or stays at home and has babies, and before you know it, there is a gap between them. Eventually the couple must work themselves back to each other or they're doomed."

"Hmm, I never thought about it quite that way," he says, as he moves on to the opposite wall. "But it's only going to get worse for the next generation as they try to do it all. I guess that's the worth of cell phones."

That conversation took place a couple of weeks ago, when working together was still a novelty. Soon into the project, however, Robin began slipping out of the house, first to his weekly golf game and then to work on publicity for his school committee campaign. Our house project, intended as something to share, is turning into more my responsibility than his. Even before the demolition, I single-handedly boxed up our library, stored our clothes in wardrobes, packed the entire kitchen, including all of our china, dishes, and glassware, and put my office to bed. Now I'm left to lug out old carpeting and woodwork on my own. I feel duped. When he donned his checked Bean jacket and duck boots to go off and chop wood during the winter months, I mistakenly thought it was a sign that he enjoyed homesteading. But now I'm beginning to think that he was just killing time until more gratifying projects came along.

The biggest blow came during one of our Chinese take-out dinners, eaten on a card table in the middle of the living room, a little more than an hour ago.

"You know all those job feelers I put out last fall and winter?" he asked, in between mouthfuls of egg foo yong.

"Yeah," I answered cautiously.

"Well, I've been nominated to be on the board of a college in Boston," he said.

"That's wonderful. What does it involve?" I asked.

"About three weekend meetings a year and sitting on a couple of committees, I imagine. The only glitch is that the first meeting is next weekend."

Quickly I thought of his other obligations, and I'm sure my face must have registered weariness, even though he just kept on eating.

"Well, then, I suppose you'll be getting out of the golf tournament," I said.

"No. That's two weekends away."

"Wait a minute," I said, coming to full attention and envisioning the calendar. "That's not the bargain we struck. We have four more weeks to have the house cleared out, and if I'm remembering correctly, you've only been partially available for the past three. Add to that two weekends and I'd say what's left of the job is going to be up to me."

"But, sweetie, these are extenuating circumstances."

I chided myself for once again believing in the illusion. Men have always fled from women — running from love affairs, off to war or meaningful professions — so much so that fleeing has become part of them. Duty to themselves, as well as desire for public importance, always seems to justify their flight.

"So I don't have your blessing?" he asked, truly not getting my fury.

"Is there a salary involved?" I asked. "Somehow that might soothe my shock." I hate that it always comes down to money, especially since last November I was extolling the virtues of volunteerism, giving back, and being generative. How easy it is to be benevolent and gracious when money doesn't matter. I certainly didn't want to begrudge him this chance for meaningful endeavor, nor did I want his optimism to dwindle, but with no money attached to any of these opportunities, I could hardly rally.

"You know, when my friend Nancy came in the other day to give me a hand, she was appalled at what you weren't doing," I inserted. I knew full well that I was "triangulating" the argument, attributing my criticism to someone else in hopes of deflecting a direct attack.

"You're always judging," he sneered, "constantly scrutinizing. I thought you'd actually applaud how things are turning out for me." He cleared away the food cartons, poured what remained of the wine in his glass, and moved toward the door. "Look, I'll be doing my share, just not on your timetable. Damn it, Joan, you're never flexible." And with that, he retreated to the only corner of the porch that hadn't been torn apart.

"Well, you're always walking away from confrontation," I shouted, "never seeing a problem through to its conclusion."

"That's because I can't stand you beating on me," he replied with disgust, and minutes later I caught sight of his back heading off down the road. Whenever we get into a discussion that he wants to win, he refuses to give an inch. This isn't a very auspicious beginning to a new life — hardly the kind of wholesome energy with which I'd hoped to infuse these walls. I sank down on the step and buried my head in my hands. Why, when I know that lashing out rarely works magic, do I proceed to do so anyway?

I fear that some improvisation on my part will be required to revive the positive momentum. As I sit outside in the dusk, my mind flashes to a friend in her second marriage who is grateful for the fact that she can finally have a temper tantrum and know that her new husband won't take it personally. Oh, c'mon, Joan, I say to myself, emotions are only imperfect thoughts anyway. Cheryl warned us that renovating a house would be hard on the marriage. Maybe working separately will be better in the long run. Since he hates instruction and craves personal freedom, maybe the key is just to back off. Why should I feel that I have to be the one making the rules around this project? If we fall behind and have to hire extra workers, that will be his problem, not mine. I shall put in just so many hours a day and leave the remainder for him. Who cares if we work side by side? That was just another one of my unrealistic, romantic notions. I've always done best in this marriage when I've taken it in measured doses, anyway.

Sitting nearby is a mass of garbage bags and milk crates that await a trip to the dump. I wander over and start to rummage through the stuff he's planning to toss out. Various and sundry broken kites, Styrofoam floats, unstrung tennis rackets, and assorted balls and bats. No problem pitching these outdated and semimeaningless items. I find an old tin of chewing tobacco, some girl's bikini bottom, one son's tackle box, an oar from their first rowboat, and some trophies won for sailboat races. Wait a minute. Wouldn't that oar look good on one of the bedroom walls, and why not display the trophies nearby on some bookshelves? We've gotten rid of so much of the house, but I can't bear to toss out these few remaining relics, nor do I want to part with the boys' faded camp T-shirts, crumpled up in the bottom of the pile.

Robin made the decision to send them to Camp Viking for sailing, and I always thought it was a good decision. "They'll learn patience and the laws of nature," he said. "When you sail, you're at the mercy of the wind. There's no quitting when you're caught in irons — you just have to wait it out and drift along."

I remember when our youngest, Luke, who could barely read and surely couldn't decipher the racecourse map, captained a little catboat and came in second. "How did you do it?" we exclaimed, in awe of his achievement. "I just watched the boat in front of me," he said, with the nonchalance of a seven-year-old.

I move to a pile of bags full of summer clothes — halter tops and shorts that no longer fit, a two-piece bathing suit, African cloth that was meant to be a sarong, tropical shirts bought on a Caribbean cruise, and a sexy black nightgown. Oh, yes, I remember that well — a good friend telling me to be naughty and sexy, that husbands love having their wives initiate sensuous romps. Back then, there were many stolen moments in the late afternoon when, after a mother's helper had collected the boys, we would make quick love, rubbing our sunburned bodies against each other, and then splurge afterward with a wine spritzer. The memory makes me smile, but then I feel sad and toss the nighty into the junk pile. I know that recollection is half invention, and yet there is hard evidence in the scrapbooks I slapped together at the end of each summer. Oh my God, where are they? I hope he hasn't tossed them away!

I dart into the cottage and locate them in cardboard boxes stashed under the stairwell. The scrapbook marked 1980 is on top with pictures from fishing expeditions, sailing races, birthday parties, and picnics at the beach. And, sure enough, there we are, Robin and I, cheering, orchestrating, and participating in it all.

It's the little details in the photographs that really grab my attention: Robin's arm around my shoulder as we watched a son race; naked Mommy with boys rinsing off the salt water and sand in the outside shower; father and sons looking for conch shells at sunset on the bay; the American flag flapping on the clothesline as a backdrop to the Fourth of July picnic. We were once those golden people in the pictures, but we are not that any longer — not better nor worse, only different. You go through certain experiences that leave a mark on you. You look back and think, I'll never be that way again. Like everybody else we are, have been, and are being tempered by life. But now, at this juncture, I find myself curiously insecure and almost frightened of the grown-up decisions to be made for the next few chapters.

"When you're growing them up," says a friend, referring to the raising of children, "you're not growing up yourself — you're merely going through the motions of being a grown-up." Her wisdom startled me. I, for one, jumped into parenthood by behaving very much like my parents did, with a modern twist or two, but certainly I didn't have the time to worry over my growth and maturity. Only recently have I had the luxury of focusing on myself. But that doesn't mean that all those years devoted to others held nothing for me. The scraps in these books feel dreamlike, as if the experiences didn't happen to me, yet that *was* my life and I *did* live it. Claim it, Joan! I tell myself. Honor the energy you gave to those years, and then use your goodness to empower the ride into the next stage.

"Never, never again," says the poet Kathleen Raine. "This moment, never, those slow ripples across smooth water, Never again these clouds white and gray . . . The sun that rose from the sea this morning will never return, for the broadcast light that brightens the leaves and glances on water will travel tonight on its long journey, out of the universe, never this sun, this world, and never again this watcher."

The sun has set long ago. The long twilight has ebbed. I wonder where Robin is and when he'll return. Looking back, the fight seems silly now, like most fights usually are. It means that we are neurotic — not a bad thing, my psychiatrist uncle tells me. Holding your own during a disagreement means that your ego is still intact — it hasn't been beaten out of you. Our aim should always be to obtain our desires.

We are two unique individuals trying to strive for meaningful existence. I need to teach my mind to accept his style. In the spirit of civility I decide to swallow further criticism and trust that he wants to contribute as much to our new life as I do. Perhaps I should simply cheer the loss of control — my failed attempt to change him, my ability to change only myself.

A brisk wind moves even the staunch pine trees, as there are rumbles and cracks of thunder. I rush toward the plank that the builders have placed by the new front door and creep gingerly up the slippery ramp. The entire past and endless future meet me in this newly created entryway that connects the old cottage to the new one. The words of Carl Jung about transition and timetables resonate within me: "The first half of life is for establishing the ego and the second half for growing into something much larger." It is time for such expansion.

As I sit here on the floor, hugging my pile full of memories, I hear a sound. It is undoubtedly a meow. "Kitty, is that you?" I look up and sure enough, a black ball of fur is scampering up the plank. Following closely behind is Robin. I scoop up the cat and go to put some milk in a bowl for her.

10

Shacking Up

JUNE

When you leave familiar ground and step off alone into a new place there will be feelings of curiosity and excitement, as well as a nagging dread. It is an experience of essential loneliness; but nobody can discover the world for somebody else. Only when we discover it for ourselves does it become common ground and a common bond and we cease to be alone.

— Wendell Berry, *A Place on Earth*

We are crowded into a Jeep — Robin, our driver Tom, and me, surrounded with duffel bags and coolers. Having packed all manner of provisions, it reminds me of going on safari in Africa, but today we are headed for the tip of Cape Cod, where we will live in a dune shack while the work on our house continues. I hold tight to the metal rod overhead to steady myself during the wild ride over the rolling and tilting plains of sand. The sea formed this landscape a long time ago as it threw itself against the coast, and the wind continues nature's work by pushing the sand into constantly changing drifts. I feel an exhilaration that comes when I break with safety and take a chance.

Unfortunately, it is a drearily gray morning, made even more ominous by the blackened skeletons of dead trees that protrude from the sandy hillsides. The setting is not welcoming; in fact, it is rather bleak and I'm having second thoughts as to whether my suggestion that we spend two weeks in a shack was a sound one after all.

I'd heard a woman lecture at the library last year about the time she'd spent in one of these remote cabins, and I had been intrigued ever since. Robin, whose tastes are more four-star than rugged, had difficulty imagining their attraction. He didn't automatically reject my idea, but he certainly had misgivings. So I tried to appeal to his sense of the unknown.

"You've always insisted that when things got dull we should have an adventure," I reminded him.

"True," he agreed, "but aren't we having one right now with the remodeling project?" I certainly couldn't argue with that answer! I finally piqued his interest by telling him the history of these structures. "They were originally constructed as shelter for shipwrecked souls — those sailors whose boats ran aground on the Race Point shoals. What's more, Eugene O'Neill wrote two of his best plays in a dune shack. And look here . . ." I said, tossing him a book, *Poet of the Dunes*. "This guy actually lived and died in one of these shacks."

"And that should entice me to go?" he quipped with a shrug of his shoulders.

"Maybe not, but how about doing it for your grandchild?"

"What? Now you've truly lost me, Joan."

"No, I'm serious. I read somewhere that Hindu philosophers suggest that prior to the birth of the first grandchild, people our age need to go into the wilderness for a period of reflection, to sift through our life experiences and develop some wisdom before the next generation arrives."

"You truly have gone over the edge," he said, but his smile was more bemused than exasperated, and a few days later we decided to give the shack a try.

That was many weeks ago, when I was feeling loose and adventuresome myself. Just now I'm overwhelmed by the remoteness of this infinite space. They don't call these dunes "the outback of the provincelands" for nothing. We are skidding through the sand as if driving in deep snow, and I wonder what Robin is thinking as he banters on with the driver about the people he brings out here and what they haul with them.

When we first started planning this foray, Robin and I made a deal: If he agreed to rough it, I would agree to cook great meals. Our cooler, now strapped precariously to the front bumper, is packed not with camp food but with delicacies — halibut, cod, chowders, filet mignon, fantail shrimp, chicken breasts. I even tucked in some caviar and smoked salmon. Behind me, our duffel bags burst with towels, blankets, and sheets, the linens cushioning numerous bottles of fine wine.

We were embarrassed by the number of bags we brought, afraid that Tom wouldn't be able to fit all of our gear into the Jeep. He seemed nonchalant and very unconcerned, telling us that one visitor carted out all her china, sterling, and glassware, and another had several satchels filled with clothing. "I still haven't figured out whom she was planning to dress for," he chuckled.

We continue for a while, silenced by the immensity of these sandy mountains, when Tom brakes and points to a distant marker: "See that pole over there," he says as we crane our necks and gape. "Directly behind it is a path that leads to the Visitor's Center. It's your quickest route to a phone. Just follow the footprints," he says, which I don't even see. He presses his foot on the accelerator and we creep onward. Although grateful for his directions, five minutes and five dunes later, I'm completely disoriented again.

For the next few miles he regales us with tidbits about this land, the history of the shack, and the joys of life in the dunes. At last, we round a bend and the Jeep labors up one last hill, sputtering and skidding all the way to the summit. "There she is!" he announces with pride, as if he's just revealed the entrance to some long-lost kingdom.

My heart sinks as I stare at a rudimentary structure tucked in a hollow, an absolutely solitary outpost. I hadn't expected a castle, but I had hoped for a view of the sea. This shack is engulfed by mountains of sand. Never mind. We had been fully informed after reading the literature sent by our landlord:

Living in a dune shack requires you to be both rugged and gentle: rugged enough to make do without necessities, and to accept whatever discomforts the dunes will deliver, yet gentle enough to live in this fragile place without damaging it. Be advised of the primitive conditions. Its physical isolation allows for uninterrupted solitude and refuge. There is no running water, telephone or electricity. In the event of an emergency you may walk to the Race Point Rangers Station to the west of the shack (about a 45 minute trek).

The present tenants, their gear packed up and piled high on the deck, wave to us eagerly. I can't decide if they are being friendly or are simply grateful to be rescued. As we pull up to the deck, hop out of the Jeep, and begin unloading our gear, they follow us around, regaling us with information and instructions about the idiosyncrasies of the shack's humble appliances. We are alerted to the fact that the tiny propane-fueled refrigerator is being temperamental, shown how to use the composting toilet, told where the grill is stored, and, finally, how to prime the pump. The shack doesn't have running water, so we will be washing our bodies and dirty dishes with what we haul up from the nearby spring that houses the shack's well.

Soon thereafter, Tom and the previous tenants are off. "See you in two weeks," he says, as he jumps into the driver's seat and pulls away.

"Well, here we are at the end of the world," I

say, opening my arms wide. "Now what do we do?"

Robin simply shrugs his shoulders. My heart beats fast and I feel a sense of impending doom, reminiscent of the time my parents first left us alone in Africa after our wedding and honeymoon. Much like then, I feel trapped and momentarily desperate. But I don't tell Robin, as I can see from his body language that he might be feeling strange as well. I remind myself that Jesus went into the desert for forty days and forty nights. I can surely handle two weeks. Besides, we've long since passed the point of changing plans. I banish further negative thoughts, offer a little prayer to ease my trepidations, and start lugging our gear into the shack.

"So what do you think?" I finally venture to ask Robin, as I unpack paper goods, pots, pans, and our favorite mugs. From his slight hesitation I think he's evading the question.

"I'm adjusting," he says, with a positive tone in his voice. "There are no reference points for this," he says. "I have nothing to compare it with."

His answer comforts me in a strange sort of way. He isn't disregarding the situation altogether, and from the tone of his voice, he seems challenged by it. We're in this together, but with separate eyes and different perspectives. Just now his optimistic outlook helps me to let go of my fear. I'm reminded of something Ann Dow said about running in the woods — that chance encounters in a natural setting can emancipate one's spirit.

The settling-in process provides me with tasks whose familiar rhythms offer some added peace. Yet the frantic pace and hard labor of the past month make coming to a halt all the more difficult. I jump when a family of mice skirt across the small kitchen counter and disappear under the window frame, then quickly hang our packaged goods in plastic bags from the rafters, and exhale. Certainly I can handle the mice more easily than the noise and dirt of our house renovation.

Someone has left a broken moon shell on the ledge over the sink. As I pick it up and look clear through to its multicolored center, I have the odd thought that Robin, by the end of our stay, will be able to see clear through me as well. The more the familiar walls of our cottage came down, the more exposed I felt, and I realized then just how much Robin and I still manage to hide from each other. Out here, we really have run out of options for avoidance. Perhaps that's been my subconscious intention — to see and to be seen. "Even love must pass through loneliness," says Wendell Berry, "setting out, not to the familiar woods of home, but to the wilderness, where renewal is found." Apprehension is only God tapping me on the shoulder. I must own this moment and go forward. With that admonition, I return to the task at hand and begin storing the potatoes, onions, nuts, and dried fruit in tins.

Slowly, gradually, the shack absorbs our belongings and we begin to take possession. I see things that make me feel more comfortable — the whitewashed walls that brighten a dingy interior on a dull day, the spatter-painted staircase that leads to the bedroom, the view of forever from the upstairs room. A map has been placed strategically on a wall near the door, and someone has marked the very spot where the shack is located. I can see where we are in relation to town, the ranger station, and two other nearby shacks. It occurs to me that the existentialist Jean-Paul Sartre would have liked such a spartan place that has little vegetation and few signs of life.

"I haven't felt this remote since Africa," I confess to Robin while scrubbing down the enamel sink, now brown from the brackish water.

"Well, certainly the chores remind me of back then," he says as he cleans the coals out of the woodstove and then heads out to lug wood in for this afternoon's fire. "We were always made to live in the future out there — preparing in advance for any catastrophe."

"Are you expecting that we'll have some here?" I ask.

"Nothing more dramatic than rain," he answers. "Although I'd feel more comfortable if we'd brought a radio so we could get a weather report."

Just now I'm also regretting my choice to opt for only natural sound, which so far amounts to listening to the wind and an occasional airplane flying overhead. Perhaps that was a mistake. But Robin's take-charge attitude offers a sense of protection. Just now I'm thinking that we were meant to partner — not go it alone. In any case, I would never have wanted to be here by myself.

"We've got a family of barn swallows living with us," Robin points out, delighted to see them taking flight and then returning again and again to the little birdhouse attached to the back of the shack.

"This part of the Cape is supposed to be a way station for migrating birds," I tell him, "and I dare say other creatures such as us! Did you see the rabbits yet? They seem to be housed in some cranberry bushes right off the deck."

Although it feels good to be noticing activity around us, I find this conversation pitiful. He's right. There are no reference points and nothing much to talk about except rabbits and birds. Fortunately, past tenants have made sure that the bookshelves are well stocked, and I peruse the collection. There are a couple of John Grisham paperbacks, a volume of John James Audubon's plant and bird drawings, an unfamiliar title by Kahlil Gibran, and most helpful, a collection of Cape Cod stories that will familiarize me with the local fauna and flora. At the very end, I find three thick journals with sketches, poems, and stories written by some of the shack's previous inhabitants. Perhaps they'll offer us some clues as to how to spend our time.

Once I've settled the kitchen and hung up my few clothes on a rafter in the bedroom, I wander out onto the deck, plop down on a crudely crafted driftwood chair, and listen to the wind. Where does it begin? I wonder. And how does a breeze whip into a storm? Such are the thoughts of a sojourner who has nothing better to do but listen for messages coming in on the wind. In time I hear faint sounds of distant society: a pounding of a hammer, the droning of a boat's engine, and the formidable voice of a man. Could we actually have a neighbor?

"Hey, Robin," I shout. "Want to find the ocean?"

He appears at the screen door and peers out at me. "Can't see why not," he answers. "We have more than enough time before dinner."

I laugh at his grim calculation and the reality that we're hard-pressed to figure out what to do with all this nothingness and freedom. "Tom said it's up thataway," I say, pointing in the direction of hovering hawks who seem to be negotiating for air space with myriad gulls. Our clothes dampen as we move closer to the sea, and our trudging becomes more labored in the loose, thick sand. I spot a forked stick, thick and thoroughly weathered, somewhat camouflaged by the silver dune grass, and grab onto it. Minutes later, I'm treated to a commanding view of the Atlantic — the blue expanse with the sea's distant rumble and soft foamy waves caressing the endless shoreline. Always at such moments I am overcome with supreme gratitude. The sky has cleared, taking the fog elsewhere, and we walk down toward the surf, somber still, but also expectant.

"Which way?" I ask. "Left takes us toward Race Point and town, right toward Truro."

"Right," he says and off we go, strolling apart, each looking for firm sand and easier walking. I'm surprised at how different everything continues to be. Even the beach is strange — the sand a dark gray rather than beige and laden with rocks, not shells. Our moods rise upon seeing a seal pop up from under the surf, and right after that Robin spots a whale spouting way off in the distance.

"The guy at the tackle store told me that Race Point was alive with all kinds of marine life," Robin says, sounding eager. "Too bad we didn't bring our tent. I could have just camped right here where there is action." We are facing seaward as a school of fish roughens the water and then flashes off again. "Damn, why didn't I think to bring my rod down with me," he says. "I never have it when the fish are around." His enthusiasm spurs me on. In some sentimental back corner of my mind, I recall the years Robin took fishing seriously — perhaps as long as twenty years ago, when he caught a twelve-pound codfish. We called in the neighbors and had a feast that very night. The taste of fresh, flaky fish was incredible.

"Supposedly the stripers are running," I say,

hoping to encourage him. "Now if you could only catch one of those." The idea of living in such a primitive way so that he could actually catch our supper intrigues me. So does spending an afternoon with binoculars searching the deep waters for whales. I haven't moved at a snail's pace for some time now, and the idea is suddenly quite appealing. So is collecting stones. I spot several lying together, as if they'd been arranged, each with a stripe down the middle. They make me think of duality, the state we are in, very much together, especially out here, and yet two individuals apart. He continues ahead of me, looking as though he's on a mission, while I amble along, beginning to finally feel I can give up the race.

Eventually the muggy air seduces me and I'm drowsy. I gravitate toward a large piece of driftwood, clear away the dried seaweed, and lie down, with the wood for a pillow. Cradled by the beach, I go limp and drift off, experiencing for the first time in weeks a sense of letting go.

I must have sensed his presence because when I come to his towering body is staring down at me. "How long have you been standing there?" I ask in a groggy, newly awakened voice.

"Just a minute or two," he says. "I must have walked forever. Saw a couple more dune shacks but they were boarded up. I think we're the only ones out here." That thought is mildly discomforting, but I counteract it by reporting on my new sense of bliss.

"Boy did I sleep . . . felt so good . . . even had a dream," I offer, still drowsy.

"Really," he says, sitting down beside me, eager to listen.

"I was in Paris, on a train or in a car, surrounded by men seemingly interested in what I was doing or saying. I joyfully announced that I want to spend a romantic day and the men laugh! That's all I remember," I say, laughing at my own absurdity.

He seems intrigued, as if he's trying to interpret the dream's meaning. We sit and stare at the swiftly increasing tide. The breakers pound onshore, licking every stone in sight, and then dragging most of them back into the depths. The next wave actually latches onto my walking stick and tries to pull it away.

"I think we should head back. It's chilly and I'm actually eager to go back to our humble home," I say, surprised at my feelings. I haul my body up from its comfortable bed, dust the seaweed off my back, grab my stick, and we begin the trek home, ambling toward the dune path, distinguishable by nothing more than a pole sticking out of the hillside.

We mount the first dune, then another, until our shack comes into view, a strangely welcoming sight as if we'd been away from home for years. After an afternoon of perfectly unprofitable idleness, we seem ready for late-day chores. I take the halibut out of the cooler, then some red potatoes, broccoli, oil, and butter. There's something about the sea air and camping out that makes me constantly famished. Robin prepares the woodstove with paper, kindling, and logs, and then hangs the Coleman lantern on a large nail hammered into the rafter over the table. The atmosphere is cozy, casual, yet special. I feel the energy returning between us.

We uncork a bottle of wine and feel the fulfillment that comes from nothing more than existence. There is a sign tacked over the front door, written on a piece of bark by one of the shack's previous occupants. It says: as is. Everything here will be just that — AS IS. What we bring to this experience or have in our possession in the way of food and clothing is all there is. As the wind whines and the shingles rattle, Robin lights the grill. I borrow a pair of his woolen socks to warm my feet and then join him beside the warm coals and watch as the waning sun casts moody shadows on the dunes.

We are two humans pared to essentials in a place devoid of excess of things other than dreams, metaphors, and wonders. Love needs space around it in order to grow. Well, we certainly have that here.

11

Safe Harbor

LATER IN JUNE

Real friendship or love is not manufactured or achieved by an act of will or intention. Friendship is always an act of recognition. When you find the person you love, an act of ancient recognition brings you together.

— John O'Donohue, *Anam Cara*

It's hot and my backpack is heavy. Still I move briskly, trudging one last time into the dunes with provisions for the day. After getting lost on my first expedition, I have become quite adept at finding my way back to the shack. I diligently follow my footprints, arrows I draw in the sand with my walking stick, an assortment of dropped reminders such as match packets, wine bottle corks, or empty soup cans, and various pieces of nautical rope I tie to tree limbs.

It has been ninety-five degrees for three days, baking me like bread. My pores ooze sweat and leave my skin encrusted in salt. The only relief, if you could call it that, is from an occasional land breeze, but it doesn't cool me off any more than would a hair dryer blowing in my face. At the moment, though, my back is pleasantly chilled by the three bags of ice I'm carrying, which hopefully will keep the scallops, shrimp, and vegetables I just bought fresh. We've lost several meals to the heat, and I've been making this trek now five days in a row.

I have the routine down pat. It takes forty-five minutes to walk from the shack to the Visitor's Center, another half hour to the little airport where our car is parked, then it's a ten-minute drive to Provincetown and the market, during which I turn on the radio and air conditioner full blast and feel like a teenager escaping in the family car. At first, it felt as though I were cheating, indulging in such creature comforts while still living the primitive life, but I've since given in to the momentary pleasure the trek affords. Today, I've tucked a local newspaper into my pack as well as Portuguese pastries and the makings for vodka and tonic. We intend to celebrate our two weeks in the bush with one last grand dinner tonight.

Although this hasn't exactly been a Sunday school picnic, it has been a chance to test our abilities to adapt, change, and thus sink deeper into each other's consciousness. There is precious little to do here except talk to God and each other, listen to ancient voices, and commune with the shack's ghosts. I often find myself on the verge of tears and have concluded that we're in a vortex, living in an altogether different frequency than ever before — that the sand which drifted to the tip of Cape Cod from faraway lands is redolent with exotic energy. These mounds contain the weight and wisdom of the ages, and we seem to be awakening to it. "What's happening to us, anyway?" Robin asked the other day, his words emerging from lips now hidden under a salt-and-pepper beard as if he were an old man from the sea.

"All our striving for presence and awareness happened quite naturally out here," I responded. "I think we're becoming drifters, like the dunes."

"Well, it did help to throw our watches away," he reasoned, "and spend our days as the weather and nature dictate."

In all the stillness, we've been learning myriad lessons and accessing many answers. For one, I decided to give up my usual questioning and bargaining, saying yes to all instincts, intuitions, and ideas, even Robin's invitations, no longer judging them.

Working in tandem has also had an impact. He willingly took on the mechanical tasks — stashing wood for the fire, priming the pump, hauling water, and filling all the kerosene lamps, while my tasks have centered on housekeeping and meals. The simplicity and necessity of our chores highlight the balance we seem to have achieved. Our beach walks have furthered our connection — meandering for hours, we search for beach glass and have collected a table full of the blue, green, brown, and white chips, a testament to time spent focused on the same activity. Even my sleepless nights, caused by the constant moan of the foghorn and the mice chasing one another around the base of our crudely constructed bed, have worked a kind of magic, forcing me into the security of his arms. I surprised myself that I need him so.

Although this vast wasteland is not exotic like Africa or Peru, it has become a place of enchantment, the desert more enticing to me now than the sea. At first the monotony of the landscape overwhelmed me, but now I'm mesmerized as the dunes are regularly reconfigured, changing color and shape at the whim of the sun, moon, and winds. I tread carefully so as not to trample the grasses that quiver in the morning and late evening, their very motion creating circular patterns in the sand, and I delight in searching for paw prints left by mysterious animals who call this space home.

I'm eager now for shade, a glass of water. I drop my shoulders and let my breath exhale through my feet for the last bit of the trek, anxious now to see my husband, but as I approach the back porch, there is no sign of him. We made a pact early on that we would each spend our days as we wished, not coaxing the other to tag along. For as the sage says, "To love is to seek to release the other." Uncharacteristically, Robin didn't want to venture very far at all; having adopted the role of purist, he hasn't wanted to run away from the isolation. I, on the other hand, unable to tame my energy, have explored every dune within a five-mile radius. I think I caught the wandering energy left behind by others who have drifted here — folks like the Puritan forefathers, Wampanoag Indians, Yankee whalers, Portuguese fishermen, and, more recently, dreamers, artists, and various other misfits.

I unlatch the crude piece of driftwood that keeps the screen door shut, lift the provisions off my back, quickly stash the ice and dinner in the cooler, and spot his note: GONE FISHING. I grab two bottles of water and head for the sea. Sure enough, as I mount the bluff, there he is, scampering about like an eight-year-old, trying to collect shiners as they flap ashore.

"Today might just be your day," I call to him as I run down the steep path toward where he stands. "Looks like you're ready to do some serious fishing," I say, gazing into the enamel bucket now heavy with bait. "I might just as well have stayed here instead of dragging myself to town to buy dinner."

"Don't be so sure," he answers, while baiting his hook. "Although they're jumping and the tide seems right, we'll still have to see." I plop down beside him and take several swallows of water. It feels good to stop and let the sun warm my rigid shoulders. While he fiddles with his gear, I luxuriate in the act of doing nothing.

"How was civilization? I can't believe you're back so soon. Did you jog?" he asks.

"Hardly. But with three bags of ice melting straight through to my T-shirt, I couldn't dally. The town was buzzing, lines of people everywhere. I think the summer people have finally arrived."

Minutes later, Robin spots a rush in the water,

a whirlpool of action, and soon thereafter, a mass of gulls and terns hover above what can only be a school of fish. He casts his line and we wait for a bite, but no luck. After several more attempts, the sea smooths out again. "Send a little prayer to Saint Anthony," I suggest. "He'll find the fish." And with that unhelpful suggestion, I tear off my shirt, pull down my shorts, and take a running dive into the water. Whoosh! The chill takes my breath away. It's as if I just dove into a bucket of ice. Are you crazy, Joan? No, just alive, I conclude, and then I swim a couple hundred strokes to get my circulation going again.

"If you don't watch out, I'll reel you in," Robin shouts, as I flip over on my back and float on the incoming tide. A small yellow airplane flies overhead pulling a banner behind that advertises a new Web site: Imagine.com.

"Hey, look at that," I shout. "You've got to imagine a bass or a bluefish circling around your bait. Either one will do," I say and then dive under again, coming up in time to ride a small wave all the way to shore. I run for his towel, wrap it around my body, and burrow my bottom in the sand. Just then Robin gets his first nibble and the duel begins. The rod bends ever so slightly, wiggling from left to right. Suddenly it collapses like a horseshoe, looking as if it is about to snap. "Hold on," I scream. "It's a big one."

Robin digs his heels into the soft shore, his jaw clenched, and begins, ever so gently, to reel and pull, reel and pull. But the fish, fighting hard now, leaps out of the water in a graceful arch, her silver and blue body shimmering from sun and water as she faces the crisis. It's strange that I find myself suddenly rooting for the fish, after wishing so hard that Robin would land one. My feelings must have something to do with staying in your element and knowing instinctively where one belongs. Then, as if wishes could be instantly granted, the line snaps, the rod straightens, and the fight is over.

"Sorry," I say through my shivers.

"Aren't you glad you didn't count on me to catch our supper," Robin mutters.

"But I do count on you for supper . . . at least to be there night after night. And tonight promises to be amazing." I continue to shiver, a strange reaction when it is so bloody hot. Or is it? "Do you feel what I feel?" I ask. "The wind couldn't possibly be shifting, could it?"

He holds out his hand. "Feels like it's coming in off the sea to me."

"But let's not get too excited. It'll take hours for this heat to blow out."

I lie back, half naked, my skin pressing against the solid warm sand, knowing that the grace of solitude and the gift of time have allowed us not to seize the day, but rather bend to its hours, turning to this or that impulse with a child's whimsy. There is a grand reward when physical sensations come unexpectedly from the earth. Although I've longed for a break in the heat, I've also learned that winds and currents can't be rushed. They have their own timetable, not unlike the natural one Robin and I have begun to develop.

We've had many adventures but none like this, where there is no destination to be sought. We were dropped into remoteness and made to coexist, and now we're seeing each other as never before. Without proper bathing facilities or all the other amenities that help perpetuate illusions, we haven't been much to look at. But surprise, surprise — we have endured! It occurs to me that so much of love is not natural. Falling in love and falling out of love happen with little assistance, but staying in love demands practice. It has felt good to get out from behind the effort and simply yield to each other. How amazing that in the meagerness of humble living, the unencumbered hours have given us the inclination to look beneath the surface of the other. As the Taoist says: "Muddy water/Let stand/Becomes clear."

I sit up and watch as he attempts one last time to hook a fish, looking like the boy I imagine he once was who would spend all day fishing on the banks of the Navesink River. As if aware of my gaze, he suddenly turns and asks, "How did I ever get here and what have I missed along the way? Fifty-five years old and it's all a blur."

"Funny you should be having that thought now. I was just getting a glimpse of the wonder you must have had when you were little. Even though I didn't know you then, I can almost guess how you must have been, and now, you have that playfulness once more."

"Perhaps, but 'I have taken too little care of this,'" he says, reciting from *King Lear*, while rubbing his tummy and then patting his heart.

"Ah yes," I say, "but Lear's other line was 'Ripeness is all.' Sure, we missed out on some of the first half of our lives as we busied ourselves with everyone else's wishes, but we've got to-morrow."

"To do what?" he asks, that old pessimism rising out of nowhere.

"To offer our uniqueness," I surprise myself by saying. "It's not what we plan to do anymore, per se, but what we intend to offer of our past knowledge, wisdom, and life experience. Above all else, it's time to imagine! It was no accident that little airplane flew overhead a while ago. In fact, I hired the pilot to do it, just for you."

He leans his rod against the bait bucket. "You jest," he says, chuckling at my lie, while embracing me from behind, then squeezing my shoulders with his strong hands. We're finding a new language with each other as tender gestures now take up where words leave off.

The gulls lift their wings in pure felicity, flying off to some faraway place, and we begin to gather up our paraphernalia and head back to the shack. "We've got to take some evening shots of our life out here," he says, "to remind us of how much we've been real together."

As we trudge through the grasses one last

time, I am overcome. I will miss this eerie world in which one of the shack's previous tenants wrote: WHERE TIME STOPS AND REAL LIFE BEGINS. How will we replicate being this wild and primitive back home?

"Time for a shower," he says, a daily treat in which I never thought I'd indulge. Each morning Robin fills the solar shower, a heavy-duty plastic bag filled with water from the pump, and then hangs it in the sun to warm. Although embarrassed at first to expose my sagging breasts and bulging belly, I now am beginning to enjoy the lack of pretense. Heat and the buildup of dirt and sweat have conspired to keep me unclothed all night and part of each day. The shedding of our clothes somehow confirms our willingness to relinquish all the old codes of conduct that kept us tight and polite.

"C'mon, you go first," he urges, "you've had the harder day." I strip and stand under the nozzle he holds over my head, melting as the soft warm water soothes my salty and sunburned skin.

"Don't be too generous. There'll be no water left for you," I caution. He squeezes the nozzle shut while I soap my arms and legs before he gives me a final rinse.

"Your turn," I say and squirt him before he's altogether naked, just like a child in a water fight. I lather his back, broad shoulders, and chest, which these days has settled nicely into his stomach. But with such a limited supply of water, our water play is over all too soon. He hands me a towel and then flops onto a chair to dry off au naturel, as a lazy breeze creeps around the corner of the shack and makes the screen door flap. "I love hearing that sound," he says. "There's something seasonal about it."

"Yep. Glad it isn't green fly season, though," I add, "especially since the screens are barely thumbtacked to the windows."

We sit in silence, staring one last afternoon at the 360-degree vista we call our yard until I break the silence. "This retreat has certainly been filled with a strange mixture of the peculiar and the superior, wouldn't you say?"

"Well, the weather was peculiar for June. It was really strange not having a sea breeze. Who would have thought that on the tip of Cape Cod the air would die?" he muses.

"Even the ocean was as still as a millpond. Don't you wish we would have had one storm," I ask, "with high winds and rain pelting on our little wood and tar-paper shack? Then we could have battened down the hatches and kept the stove burning, working as a team to ward off the elements. At the very least, it would have felt like company."

"Yeah, but we were working as a team doing our own chores," he argues. "And actually, I don't think this little shack could withstand much wind and rain. A storm might have finished us. But you're right; it would have been an

211

adventure. And I did bring layers of clothing for any eventuality."

"Then again, we wouldn't be sitting around like this," I suggest, opening my towel and exposing my body. "Too bad we can't be naked all the time," I continue, running a comb through my gnarly hair before putting it behind my ears. I catch a twinkle in his eye and feel momentarily sexy.

"I've been meaning to tell you how great you look with your hair pulled back," he says with a wistful tenderness, "especially when you put it in a rubber band on top of your head." He reaches over and pushes a loose end off my forehead, and I feel noticed, his small gesture carrying with it comfort.

Again silence, before more goose bumps and the arrival of a swarm of mating bees, hardly interested in us, but annoying enough to make Robin suggest we duck inside. "I'm going to really dress for dinner," he announces.

"You're what?" I ask. Do I have anything in my duffel in order to do the same? I did pack a black-and-white sundress for reasons unknown. That will have to do. I head for the loft and catch my image as I pass by a mirror. Actually, I don't look half bad, even though I boast only a windblown hairdo, and any semblance of makeup has been replaced by freckles and a tan. I rummage through my bag, now full of soiled clothes, in search of the dress. In the process, I find a poem obviously intended to be read here, or perhaps its sentiments simply reflect wishful thinking.

> *Blessed are the man and woman*
> *who have grown beyond their greed*
> *and have put an end to hatred,*
> *no longer nourishing illusions*
> *but delight in the way things are*
> *and keep their hearts open, day and night.*
> *They are like trees planted near flowing rivers*
> *which bear fruit when they are ready.*
> *Their leaves will not fall or wither.*
> *Everything they do will succeed.*

"No longer nourishing illusions . . . but delight in the way things are . . ." That has been the miracle that found us. I slip on my dress, grab my gold scallop-shell earrings left in my bag from another trip, step into black sandals, and head down the stairs to begin preparing dinner.

The shack, enveloped in filtered, late-afternoon light, would be perfect just now for a *House & Garden* magazine shoot. Never mind the broken-down furniture covered with someone's old sheets, or the round table painted a dark green with mismatched captain's chairs on either side. The decorative deficiencies of this place have forced us to infuse it with our own brand of creativity.

We've gotten into the habit of preparing the entire dinner while there is still plenty of light and then we retire to a dune or the porch for cocktails. Tonight's entrée is seafood pasta. I chop plenty of garlic, onion, and parsley, sauté it in olive oil, add some clam juice and white wine, and let it simmer while I set the table with the shack's mismatched plates. Finally, I grab the bluefish pâté and head out to Robin, who is already situated on a dune we've named Sunscape, because it catches the last rays of the day. He's brought a milk crate and covered it with a dish towel to fashion a table for our hors d'oeuvres.

"Here's to the chill in the air . . . finally!" Robin says, lifting his blue plastic goblet toward the sky.

"You know, I'm going to miss drinking out of plastic and eating off paper."

"You can rest assured, sweetie, that our cottage won't be entirely ready when we return. I think we'll be camping out a while longer."

"I'm glad we held back as much as we did during the planning with Cheryl. After these weeks of spartan living, it would feel strange to return to an overfinished house. Not that I want to live like this all the time, but life is too full of material things, don't you agree? The unfinished look has far more appeal."

"Does that mean you won't be buying new furniture?" he's quick to ask.

"Maybe a few pieces, especially for the new kitchen. Otherwise, we'll make do. I've enjoyed living without excess. You know what I mean."

"Not really," he answers.

"Being free of nonessentials like the news, television, the stereo, and all the appliances, we've had to fill the void, entertain ourselves and each other, and, best of all, listen."

"We sure don't play Scrabble at home. I've been keeping a running tally of our nightly games."

"I didn't know. I suppose you're winning, right?"

"How did you guess?"

"I may be a woman of words, but you're the strategist at Scrabble. Never mind. I've still got tonight to make up the difference."

I lean back against a pile of sand. With clouds moving in, the sky will soon be spectacular — deep blue, purple, shocking pink, and a tinge of orange. "Remember our first night, when you discovered this dune, and we sat here so very disoriented, not knowing if it was Saturday night or not? We couldn't begin to imagine what we were going to do with ourselves for two whole weeks!"

"And we thought we'd made an awful mistake by coming," he adds.

"Well, was it as good for you as it was for me?"

"Depends upon what aspect we're talking about," he says, leaving me to guess where he found his bliss. "I surprised myself that I could be satisfied with such simplicity. Do you remember asking me last winter if I had a hard time being present and conscious?"

"I sure do. And you thought I was talking about awareness. Seems to me you thought the entire subject to be too much like work," I remind him.

"Well, out here, I was finally able to grasp the importance of what you were getting at. It's as if I've gotten down on all fours and inspected every damn piece of sand. And what's more, I'm the better for it, because I've truly known these days. Want a refill?" he asks, noticing our empty glasses. As I hand him mine I offer him my cheek to be kissed.

"Later," he says, sliding down the dune and heading toward the shack.

"Later is a dreadful word," I call after him, raising my voice a bit to make sure he gets the message. "Not much different than saying no. Saying yes may circumvent the immediate action, but it always leads to diversion and fun."

As the crickets begin their evening lullaby and fireflies light up the grass like twinkle lights at Christmas, everything seems soft and dreamlike. I feel sated, knowing that slowly, gradually, we've been found by the other. This spiral spit of land has brought us back to center. Whether it was instinct that directed us here or a complete accident, we've both ripened and weathered, not unlike the shack.

He returns several minutes later, the sun creating a glow on his tanned forehead. I like the way his bright blue sweater complements his scruffy beard. I motion for him to snuggle next to me in the crevice I've widened to accommodate two. "Too many people run away from loneliness the moment it seems strange or awkward," Joan Erikson once told me. "Yet happiness has to do with patience and presence. It's about intention — wanting it and being ready to accept love when it arrives."

"Nothing did go as we expected, did it?" I say. "And yet, things conspired to make it perfect, somehow."

"Are you referring to this little adventure or our entire marriage?" he asks.

"I suppose a little of both. I think these shifting sands were meant to be a theme for us. Not that we intentionally came out here for life lessons, but we're leaving with such a powerful image of how things change and yet remain ongoing."

"You're not going to get existential on me, are you?" he asks.

"Would I do that?" I say, cocking my head in a coy way, and then slipping my bare foot in between his legs.

"You used to do this at every dinner party we ever went to," he says while squeezing my toes. "I never quite knew what to do."

"Oh yes you did," I answer. "You obliged, like now. I was always testing to see if you were there with me or not."

"Oh, really. I suppose I must be grateful that it was my lap in which you were placing your foot and not someone else's."

The evening begins to turn in on us, the long twilight has ebbed. The barn swallows have long since tucked into their shelter, while our family of rabbits now trusts us enough to scamper onto the porch. "The wind has picked up, sweetie. Time to go inside," he says, interrupting my pleasure.

"Just a few more minutes," I beg. As the outhouse door bangs against the side of the shack and the foghorn begins to moan, I feel blessed, sitting here with my best friend — two souls who have known each other suddenly experiencing a deeper recognition.

The theologian Frederick Buechner said: "You can survive on your own; you can grow strong on your own; you can prevail on your own; but you cannot become human on your own." We wanted to leave a mark on the world, when perhaps the greater achievement is that we have left a mark on each other. Now, with youth and the need for clearly defined goals behind us, we're aiming for the whole of life again. He extends his hand and pulls me up from my soft seat. I feel an overwhelming sense of gentleness.

12

Forever at Sea

LATE JULY

At sea, the motion never stops.
Slowly your body develops a
rhythm with the boat. Your
cluttered world narrows to the
simplicity of sky, wind and sea.
Slowly you become still.

— David Treadway, *Dead Reckoning*

There is only one salve available to me when I am in need of exorcising a bad dream — take flight, get out from under, go to a place where my mind will expand rather than contract. That is why, during the wee hours of this morning, I find myself driving toward Hardings Beach, a place surrounded on three sides by water, with vast moors and a defunct lighthouse at its point.

I'm not at all surprised that my nightmares have disrupted my sleep since our return home from the dune shack. Reentering civilized life after living in an uncomplicated world has been unsettling, not the least of all because the cottage is still in an unfinished state. Our private space is filled with workers, ordinary daily routines are in disarray, and we are constantly confronted with trivial decisions like which faucet or light fixture to purchase.

In the nightmare, I was wandering through endless hallways with numerous doors, all of which were closed and locked. Trapped and with no exit, I was confused about how I got there and how I was meant to get out. No wonder I awoke baffled and anxious, haunted by the thought that perhaps redoing the cottage and settling down once again represent — to me, anyway — no light at the end of the tunnel. But wasn't I a willing participant in all of these plans? Haven't I been eager to design a shared future? Maybe my old neurosis is rearing its ugly head — the negative voice that insists when things are going well, tragedy is sure to strike. Perhaps my feelings are further complicated by the fact that it happens to be our thirty-second wedding anniversary.

I squint against the early-morning sun as it hits the windshield and, pulling down the visor, creep along at a snail's pace. Usually it is fog that inhibits travel at this hour of the morning; today, which is predicted to be a scorcher, it is the sun. I grab a cup of coffee to go at a favorite hangout, too late to catch my fishermen friends who have long since launched their boats and most likely cast their nets by now. But I'm not interested in socializing with anyone but myself.

Back in the car and nearing the shore, my mood lifts along with the mist as it rises over a meadow of cornflowers and clover. The beach at dawn heralds a new beginning — a surefire way to soften senses gone brittle during the night. This has always been a place that offers comfort and inspiration: a beach so expansive that even the most closed person is opened upon arrival. It was here that I came, upon arriving at the Cape for my year alone; where I brought Joan Erikson numerous times on treasure hunts for our souls; and where, in the dead of winter, I brought Robin, when both our relationship and the sea were frozen. Somehow, the purity of the place helped to soften us up.

I suspect that the lighthouse, just now a tiny speck far off in the distance, contributes to my attraction to this beach, standing as it does at the tip of the harbor, a landmark and safety valve that people of the sea depend upon to find their way home, and from which people like me draw strength.

I step out of the car and stretch, as a lazy breeze blows through me. Instead of walking, I sink into the nearest dune to drink my coffee and am hit with a cavalcade of smells — soggy salty air, dried pine, a stench from broken snail shells, perhaps even some dead fish. Nearby are six or seven other early risers — people bent on sampling a summer's day, taking from it what they wish. There are two kayakers, their sleek vessels skimming across the surface of the smooth sea, one jogger, a fly fisherman, and some shell seekers. I hear the kayakers babbling to each other, a lilt in their voices, some laughter and lightness, and I immediately envy their adventure.

Come to think of it, I haven't been particularly whimsical lately. In fact, since breaking my ankle, I've been more homeward than outward bound, living mostly in the future, and since our time in the dunes we have gotten caught up in the cottage, which has more to do with the future than the here and now.

Perhaps the nightmare was meant as a warning — don't get boxed in, provide yourself with choices and alternatives — but then there's always the thorny issue of money. Having dumped most of the profit from the sale of our New York house into the cottage, I'm worried that there won't be any left over for travel and discovery. Hadn't we hoped to live in different countries for a month at a time when we retired? Is that fantasy and others like it no longer an option?

Well, we could at least invest in a couple of kayaks and maybe some new bicycles. I did have the idea that we would share a sport together, perhaps even do some long-distance hiking. We must be careful not to lose sight of our dreams in favor of the stability of day-to-day life. What's more, we need to hold back a portion of our days for each other, not just mealtimes.

I recently asked Robin how much we were worth. He immediately began talking about real estate holdings and our stock portfolio. "No, I'm asking you how much what we've created together is worth."

"Oh," he said, nonplussed. "There aren't words that can place a value on us," he continued. "Rather than me judging our worth, perhaps it is our children and their children who should make that judgment."

"Still, I want to hear it from you," I probed.

"Well, I made a commitment," he answered,

matter-of-factly. "The way a man honors his marriage tells you something about how he will honor other large commitments in his life."

"Does it have anything to do with love?" I asked, fishing for more.

"I can't imagine living with anyone else, if that's what you mean," he continued, using his words sparingly.

"Could you elaborate?"

"Have you forgotten what brought us together?" I searched my mind for an answer. "If you recall, I thought you were outrageous that day when I spotted you in the Green Room at Yale — dressed in your long green skirt, loud, glamorous, and very attractive. But what really did it was that Pinter play, *The Room*, in which we played an elderly couple who never communicated."

"You're kidding! All I can recall about that show is that it was a theater-of-the-absurd play, and we struggled to understand the layers of Pinter with all his pregnant pauses. His form and style went way beyond anything I had ever done previously. And the director! He didn't have a clue either."

"But that was the unifying element," Robin insisted, "figuring out how my character related to yours . . . all those hours of rehearsal time in each other's apartments. Besides, it was essentially my debut at Yale Drama School. You had already done a big show with Stacy Keach. I had a lot to live up to."

"Really," I countered, intrigued now as he was detailing so much of our ancient history.

"In the process we began to discover each other. Acting is, after all, about dropping one's defenses," he said. "Certainly you know that."

"Yes, but I think it's amusing that we were working in a genre where the characters never do understand one another. They're only interested in their own reality and hardly ever tune in to anyone else's."

"Ah, yes," he continued, "but struggling with a role, any role, whether it's on stage or off, tends to move the participants to another level. Perhaps we were in training back then for growing old together," he quipped.

My mind wandered to Joan Erikson once again, when she explained to me that the most compassionate people in real life are those who did a lot of playacting as children. "You're required to understand the motivation behind another's actions," she said, "and to have sympathy for their plight. Along the way an enormous compassion develops."

As if for the first time, I saw her truth and how compassion had seemingly been an underlying strength in Robin's and my relationship.

"Well, that was it for me, anyway," Robin said, breaking into my silence. "From the beginning we seemed to be practicing connection. I was certainly in need of that, coming as I did from a family where very little substance passed between anyone. I suppose I was longing for an intimacy, sharing thoughts and feelings. I got that from you."

"You probably got more than you bargained for in that department," I said, making us both dissolve into a full-bodied laugh. "But what about passion? I heard someone define love as a temporary madness that subsides. Do you ever wish for some of that madness back again?"

"Hell, that's all illusion," he answered as if he knew and didn't much care.

"Don't you miss desire?" I continued.

He didn't miss a beat. "We have that, don't you think? The word doesn't always have to have sexual connotations. Right now, desire for me means spending the rest of my life with a good friend and confidante."

"Really?" I answered, taking this remarkable compliment and tucking it away while closing the file on this moment. If I was looking for romance, I had just found it.

The memory of that conversation offers as much of a tonic as this beach does, both quelling my anxiety, at least for the moment. Now it's time to hit the road. Quickly, I'm up and off to the lighthouse, taking the path that cuts through the center of this peninsula, walking with the dunes and Nantucket Sound on my right and an inlet with marsh and moors on the left. I pass several patches of Queen Anne's lace misted up among clumps of cornflowers, both bending in the breeze. Without thinking, I pick a bunch of cornflowers and then remember that once they are picked they change altogether, even their color fades. I suppose none of us should allow anyone to pluck us from our roots — from that which grounds us and makes us whole. Robin hasn't done that to me, nor I to him. We seem to have gravitated to a common ground where each of us can flourish.

Is that the worth of our union? Perhaps. But it also has to do with the realness Robin thought we had achieved at the dune shack. Authentic relationships have a way of forcing the two individuals involved to become witnesses for one another. We weren't always so free-floating and natural, but this year, it seems, we've become each other's sanctuary, ever so slowly creating a refuge in which we are free to craft our spirits.

I recall a scene from a children's book, *The Velveteen Rabbit,* in which two stuffed animals discuss this very thing. " 'You BECOME,' the horse said to the rabbit. 'It doesn't happen all at once. It takes a very long time. Generally by the time you are REAL most of your hair has been loved off and your eyes drop out and you get loose in the joints and very shabby. But those things don't matter, because once you are real, you can't be ugly, except to people who don't understand.' "

For sure, I no longer want him to be anything other than what he is, and I suspect he feels the same about me. It is such a relief, not having to become more or different or reach for characteristics that are beyond our grasp. We've been called to start anew — to let go of the worn-out expectations and accept the person we wake up beside each day for who we are that very morning.

I pass great patches of ripening beach plums, hanging heavy on their branches. They have gone through their complicated metamorphosis — first bursting forth with pink and white blossoms, then letting their petals blow off to expose small green buds that soon swell and turn yellow, then orange, and finally, a pungent crimson. Summer is at its sweetest by the end of July when growth is steady, everything is at its fullest, and there seems to be an open invitation to celebrate things ripening. Didn't I revel in becoming a ripened woman last year? Now it seems to be the time to relish ripening relationship. Ours has blossomed ever so gradually, not unlike the beach plums on the vine or the gentle rise of the tide in the marsh nearby, creating a stream that is curling through the lush grasses. Where once there was a mudflat, now it becomes a burgeoning series of tributaries and channels.

Walking jauntily now, I hear seven or eight different birdcalls — the air containing a melody all its own — and I want to join in, singing aloud a favorite hymn: "Spirit, spirit of gentleness, blow through the wilderness, calling and free. . . . Spirit, spirit of restlessness, stir me from placidness, wind . . . wind on the sea."

From nightmares to daydreams — a bad dream banished by little more than the effort it took to get out of bed and embrace life at the sea-shore. I suppose the future will always seem sur-real, since I cannot predict what it will bring until it arrives, and so it remains, like a Dalí painting — wild, frightening, and elusive. The lesson, of course, is to stay in the present but welcome change. "Changelessness is death," the Chinese proverb cautions.

Perhaps that is why I was led to this particular beach today — a place where I can watch begin-nings and endings merge. Somewhere way off shore the sea joins with Nantucket Sound as un-known currents blend together and then swish into the harbor and back out again. Ebb and flow, that is the message. "Tide and time wait for no man" — or woman, for that matter. I stand here, listening only to the gentle lapping of water and am once again at peace.

I circle around the entire point, then up through the dune grass as if I knew there would be a path that leads back to the road. Sure enough, I find a narrow strip of sand and hightail it back to the car. Eight thirty-five, the clock on the dashboard says as I turn on the ignition. It seems eons of time have passed since I slipped out of bed in my unquiet state. I'm anxious to get home now, having forgotten to leave Robin a note of my whereabouts. What's more, I didn't even consider that it was our anniversary when I left. Most days, it wouldn't matter to him where I'd gone, but just now I'm feeling a bit contrite, caught up by my momentary thoughtlessness.

He's sitting on the front porch in a newly purchased rocking chair as I pull up to the cottage. Grace is imminent. I now hold a passionate belief in reinvention.

"Happy anniversary," he shouts, before I'm even out of the car. I walk briskly and bend over to give him a kiss. "I can't believe it — thirty-two years with the same person! It's almost ridiculous," I jest.

"But that's just it," he answers, solemnly. "We're not the same person."

Acknowledgments

I offer gratitude to my editor, Gerry Howard, for his literary insight and strong support of the subject matter; Anne Merrow, for her critical eye and keen editorial suggestions; Heather McGuire, for her enthusiasm and tenacity in marketing the concept of being unfinished to women nationwide; Oprah Winfrey for broadcasting the issue of marriage sabbatical nationwide and the importance of individual space in every union; Olivia Blumer, my agent, who because of her expertise and loyalty was able, once again, to find the right home for this book; and most especially Rebecca Anderson, my anchor, friend, helpmate, and mentor in all things literary.